toddalicious

a travel blog and photo adventure
by todd shaver

To my Uncle Steve,
who inspired everyone he knew with a sense of adventure

To my mom,
who taught me to find the magic in the small things

And to my dad,
who's always been there to support me

Thank you all.

contents

introduction

After I graduated from college in 2009, I bummed around a bit looking for a job. What I really wanted was to find a job in Southern California, near where I had gone to college. However, after looking for quite a while, I ended up being offered a job in my small hometown of Modesto, in California's Central Valley.

This was great for a while, and I made some great connections and friends. But I'm afraid this is a bit of a cliché story – after 5 years of working in an office I quit. It was a mixture of me being bored from being in the same place for 5 years, and a need to part ways with my employer. But I also had some important people in my life awake within me a desire to see more of what life had in store. I'd always been afraid of uncertainty, and had felt a desire to live a predictable, stable life.

So, like I said, I quit. It's easy to have in mind the things you'd like to do, but it's harder to do them. Seeing New Zealand had been a dream of mine for years, and one night – on a whim – I checked the airfare. What I found was a screaming deal, about HALF of the typical cost. And thus began the adventure.

New Zealand was to be the first stop, but there was also another item to cross off of my bucket list – the John Muir Trail in the Sierra Nevadas. I had seen the signs growing up in Yosemite, the ones that say "Mt. Whitney: 211 miles," and had always laughed, thinking they were some kind of joke or something. Walk two hundred and eleven miles? Who does that? But later on in my life, hearing stories from my aunt who had done a portion of it with her sister, I was intrigued by the concept of a backpacking trip long enough to need a resupply. And the seed was planted.

But, after I jumped through all the hoops to get a permit for the incredibly popular JMT, I realized it wasn't big enough. Two weeks? I would be able to get two weeks off of work to hike a trail while employed. While I was unemployed, I needed to dream bigger. For some reason, it was only a short jump in my mind to go from 2-3 weeks on trail to 4 months, and after all, the PCT *includes* the JMT. Slam dunk, right? And PCT permits are much easier to obtain, and free. My mom, bless her heart, has learned to expect a little crazy from me, and volunteered to be my support person on the ground while I was hiking.

Through a mixture of a desire to share my experiences with others and a need to keep my family updated on my location and safety, I elected to keep an online journal, a blog, which I've now converted to print.

I had an internal struggle while I was out traveling. I wanted to take pictures to share all of the amazing vistas and experiences I had with those I care about, but at the same time I didn't want to share the pictures. Why not? Because I was afraid the pictures might act as a substitute for the real thing – if you see the pictures you might assume that you've now seen that place. They're not substitutes - they should be enticing tidbits. In the same way that a snack isn't a meal, but only serves to get your mouth watering in preparation for the REAL food, my hope is that these stories and pictures don't satisfy your desires for adventure but inspire you to live your own adventures.

Bon appétit, and bon voyage!

-Todd "Shade" Shaver

prologue: end of an era
bike tour up the california coast

out on the open road!

april 20, 2015

Freedom at last! Had some good years behind a desk, but finally said goodbye. Wasted no time hitting the open road. Chuck and I strapped our stuff to the back of our bikes and headed north for a "short" four-day tour north up the California coast. In typical fashion, "ride creep" got in the way of an on-time departure and we took off like a herd of turtles at the early hour of 7:45pm. Let's just say that it's a good thing we don't run an airline company. Or a public transit company.

Anyway, we were all too happy to use our (now favorite) cheap Chinese headlights that are AMAZING! I was tasked with route finding north from Sunnyvale to Marin Headlands, and I failed. I tried the inland bay route, and it was full of rough roads, bad bike paths, stop lights, and the lack of bike lanes. But, like good little bike tourers, we rolled into our awesome free Marin Headlands campsite at 2am. Day's total: 61 mi

Next day we started earlier (11am, lol) and headed up Hwy 1 all the way to Monte Rio, on the Russian River. We passed through this delightful little town called Freestone just south of Occidental, it was beautiful! At Occidental we started tracing the route of the Levi Gran Fondo, and I have to say, everything I've heard about how beautiful those roads are is true! We ran into one of the "locals" (read: homeless) in Monte Rio before setting up camp, and had a very…interesting conversation.

For about an hour. It started out fairly normal, before he started talking about his ability to make atomic bombs with his poop and how God had cut off his head, played with it, and then given it back to him. I digress. Stealth camping along the Russian River is superb, and we had a great evening ☺ Day's total: 72 mi

Next day had us head north past Cazadero, onto King Ridge, and down the epic descent of Meyer Grade, back down to Hwy 1. From there we started heading south. And we just kept pedaling. And pedaling. Until, *pffffFFFFFTTTTtttt*…first flat of the trip. Chuck, who in true form was using a 23c road racing tire pumped to 145psi to carry 250lbs of body and gear, had gotten a sizable slice in his sidewall. As he sat down, I decided to check the map. And realized we were not where we thought we were. Hwy 1 had turned right a LONG time ago, and we had not. We were 5 miles from Petaluma, so I called a friend in Petaluma, we had some dinner,

Chuck and Todd about to head out on bikes!

Stealth camping on the Russian River.

Made a friend…and got some life advice ☺

4

Look at that magnficent steed! (That's right, I called it a "steed") oh yeah, there's some pretty nature behind it too. Near King Ridge.

California's coast sure does have the epic vistas! Atop Meyer Grade.

Chuck couldn't resist getting friendly with the cows and taking some glamour shots.

On the other side of Chuck's lens...

Seriously, at some point I'ma run out of new words to use in describing epic vistas.

and we slept on a dry couch as it rained outside ☺ Day's total: 86 mi

Next day was the longest day: we had to get from Petaluma to Sunnyvale, about 94 miles. Undeterred, we got to work, and took D Street out of Petaluma into the most beautiful scenery ever. This was the second time on this trip that I had to adjust my definition of "most beautiful roads I've ever cycled on." Seriously. I highly recommend checking this place out. We stopped just past Fairfax for a snack stop, but after a lovely conversation with a man in town, we were required to backtrack to what was claimed to be the best ice cream ever. Oh, and burgers.

We were not disappointed in the ice cream. Never have I tasted lavender ice cream with such amazing flavor! Check out the "Fairfax Scoop" if you're in the area.

Then, as if our mileage wasn't enough already, we got to the Golden Gate Bridge and Chuck suggested we climb

It's a good thing Chuck got a flat, or we might never have realized we were off course!

So I'm convinced that at least half of being a successful restaurant owner is thinking of witty food item names. Reminds me of "Bob's Burgers" ☺

Oh my gosh if you haven't been out in this area on a bike, get out there. Like now. Go do it. See that smile on my face?

Hawk Hill to pad our elevation numbers a bit. Definitely worth it! After that, it was Chuck's turn to route find through the city, and he did a much better job than I. We went down the ocean side of the city, and apart from lots of sand blowing in from the beach, it was flat with a solid tailwind. At some point we realized that, if we hurried, we could get to our favorite restaurant before they close! From there on out, it was a hammer fest. And you can bet, with the promise of salmon burritos, we made it with 20 mins to spare. Day's total: 104 miles

At the top of Hawk Hill, all the hard work paid off.

chapter 1: the land of the long white cloud

exploring new zealand

New Zealand at a glance. Because you can totally understand a country based on numbers, right?

	New Zealand	California
Total Area	268,021 km²	423,970 km²
Percent Water	1.6	4.7
Population	4.6 million	38.8 million
Population Density	17.2/km²	95/km²
Age	European Gov't: May 7, 1856	Statehood: September 9, 1850
Highest Point	Mt. Cook: 3,724 m (12,218 ft)	Mt. Whitney: 4,421.0 m (14,505 ft)
Largest City (pop)	Auckland: 1,454,300	Los Angeles: 3,928,864
Miles of Freeway (Motorway)	199 km (123.7 mi)	19,304.9 km (11,995.50 mi)
Protected Areas (parks, forests, reserves)	30% of the country	46.7% of the state
Number of Sheep	39 million	600,000
Number of Cows	6.4 million	5.2 million

first few days in nz
may 2, 2015

Well, I'm really here! Doesn't really feel like I'm on the other side of the globe. I just went to sleep, and woke up…somewhere else lol. The flight on AirNZ was awesome. All the flight attendants had very dapper outfits, accented with purple and the AirNZ logo pattern, and when we boarded every seat had a blanket, pillow, and headphones waiting. I was also surprised when they announced that there would be two complimentary meal services during the flight, as well as complimentary wine! So much for me planning ahead and bringing along a burrito for the flight. But don't worry, it got eaten ☺

Auckland feels like the "smallest" big city I've been in. It's clean, doesn't smell bad, is very well taken care of, but is totally walkable in size. I was totally surprised how much of an Asian population there is here though! About two-thirds of the shops we passed on the bus ride into town were Asian, and I wasn't able to find a western supermarket, only like 15 Asian supermarkets. Guess I'll be having Asian food for dinner for the next couple nights ☺

The rain is pretty silly…the weather will be fine, and then all of a sudden it'll start pouring for 5 minutes, and then it'll stop. I think it rained like 4 or 5 times today ☺

I saw all I wanted to see of the downtown pretty quickly, I'll be happy to get out into the country.

Couldn't help myself. Anyone else see the irony here? I have to imagine they could have thought of a different brand name if they were gonna advertise "real" juice. Who ever heard of a "real McCoy"?

Auckland has its own space-needle like structure. But don't be fooled by the freeway…most of the roads here are two lane, lol.

top 10 ways to not look like a n00b while traveling nz

may 3, 2015

Okay, no pictures for you guys this time, but I present to you some sage advice. I've made these mistakes so you don't have to, because I'm just that kind of guy (the kind of guy who makes mistakes).

1. **Dunedin is pronounced "dun-eden" not "doon-uh-din."** Apparently this is obvious to everyone except me.

2. **When walking on the sidewalk, step left instead of right to avoid people.** I can grasp the concept of driving on the wrong side of the road, but it's the instinctual stuff that gets me. Everyone thinks backwards here.

3. **Remember that, to the rest of the world, saying the temp is 85° at home doesn't make sense.** You'll get a very confused look unless you also think in Celsius.

4. **Actually SPEND the $1 and $2 dollar coins.** Pocket change here is actually functional. And heavy.

5. **Pretend like you don't care if your bus leaves without you.** Nothing is more n00bish than running to the bus stop with a fully loaded pack. Looking cool, and sauntering instead, is definitely worth the added risk. Actually, let's generalize here. Don't appear too excited about anything. This is closely related to the cyclist's concept of "tranquilo."

6. **New Zealand is NOT the land down under.** Don't ever confuse them with Aussies, you shall be swiftly rebuked.

7. **Try to avoid saying Māori place names.** But if you must, break it into 2 or 3 letter syllables each ending with a vowel, and say it syllable by syllable with no emphasis on any syllable.

8. **Don't snicker when you hear a Māori place name involving kaka, titi, or pupu.** I know it's tough, but let's at least TRY to be respectful here.

9. **Wear impractical clothing for a rainy climate, like cotton.** It's fashionable, nothing else matters. Also, wool is still oddly expensive even though the sheep to people ratio must far exceed unity by now.

10. **Don't try to explain to people how not to be a n00b when you're still clearly a n00b.**

top 10 weird words

may 3, 2015

Okay, so I knew coming here that there would be some different words. New Zealand does have ties to the UK after all. But apart from some ones I expected, like "digestives" for cookies, here are some oddities. This is subject to addition as I continue.

1. **Hire = rent.** This threw me for a loop at first, as how can you "hire a suit" or "hire a bike"?

2. **Petrol = gas.** Okay, so this isn't super weird. But I can't get used to saying petrol.

3. **Meths = alcohol (denat).** Sooo…meth in the states means something you definitely wouldn't want to get caught with. But many backpackers use it for stoves.

4. **Trundler = shopping cart.** Yeah, so I think in the UK they call them trolleys? But trundler? Either that's silly or endearing, haven't decided.

5. **Car park = parking lot.** I envision something like a "dog park" with cars able to run around freely, and play around with other cars. But alas, it's much more boring than that.

6. **Motorway = highway/freeway.** Motorway gives me images of some sort of racetrack speedway. But really it's just like a two lane highway.

7. **Backpacker = hostel.** Sure, hostel means hostel here too, but I've never heard them referred to as "backpacker's." Very cool that there are so many of these, and they are often pointed out on the streetsigns from the center of town.

8. **Tramping = backpacking.** A lot of these words just have weird connotations to me…isn't tramping something you wouldn't want to do to nature? Regardless, they've got a lot of it, and they make it so accessible to the public.

9. **Panel beater = body shop.** So this one makes more sense to me than the American version, as it actually explains what it is.

10. **Flat white = latte.** Okay, so this needs some explanation. A flat white is like neither a latte nor a cappuccino, but better than both. It is a specialty here, with two shots espresso and steamed milk. There is very little foam, and it comes in a much smaller cup than a latte so it has a much higher ratio of espresso to milk. It is spectacular.

auckland to dunedin

may 3, 2015

So, I'll keep the chatter here to a minimum and just throw up a bunch of pictures onto the page. Auckland was a typical big city in feel with skyscrapers and fancy shops downtown, being New Zealand's biggest city. But it was the smallest big city I've experienced. Kind of a cool juxtaposition. I only spent a day there, and wanted to hurry down to the South Island both to catch a rugby game in Dunedin and see the mountains before the winter set in too far.

I was able to stack my ferry and bus connections and get all the way to Dunedin in three days! Although I blazed right on through Christchurch going south, it was my favorite so far of New Zealand's big cities, so I'd love to go back. It has an interesting story – a few years back the city was devastated with earthquakes and like a full year of aftershocks. A bunch of people left the city, and they're still rebuilding. I didn't get quite so lucky with connections past Dunedin, so I spent a couple days there. Dunedin seems a little older, and reminds me very much of 19th-century european architecture. They are home to a Cadbury manufacturing plant as well as a claimant to the steepest street in the world.

I met up with a friend of a friend of a friend, for a small music show at a bike shop. This guy had packed up his stuff into a bike trailer (guitar, amp, etc) and cycled the whole length of New Zealand playing shows the whole way. Really good music too!

I guess I should make an occasional appearance in these pics.

Heading down to the South Island.

The bike touring musician!

An excellent handmade vegan burger at a farmers market in Dunedin.

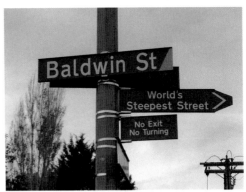

Dunedin's claim to fame.

Dunedin's got some big, old, cool looking buildings!

I guess you know it's steep when the sidewalk turns into stairs.

The view from the top of Baldwin St.

Rugby at the Forsyth-Barr stadium in Dunedin.

Aaaand caught the rugby game I'd been looking forward to. "We" crushed South Africa handily!

After this, it's off to Te Anau and some nature and mountains!

mountain time!

may 9, 2015

After a couple days in Dunedin, I caught a bus in the evening out to Te Anau – the gateway to the Fiordlands. The people disembarking the bus with backpacks all kind of looked at each other and asked each other where we were all staying for the night. One couple had booked a room at a local backpacker, so we all followed them in a small herd, checked in and ate dinner together. One of the guys and I decided to head out to the Kepler Track bright and early. This was the first Great Walk track for both of us, so we weren't quite sure what to expect in terms of maps and equipment required, but we agreed to just wing it and not wait until the visitor center opened at 8:30 to ask.

This beach along Lake Te Anau sure makes NZ feel like a Pacific island!

The Luxmore Hut, on the Kepler track. Really impressed by the quality of the tracks, and the huts! Very welcome when it's (often) raining outside.

On the Kepler Track, looking towards Lake Te Anau.

Birds in flight over the Kepler Track. Curiously, so far birds are the only wildlife I've seen here.

See? I really was here!!

The Kepler Track was so unique! For the middle portion it literally went along a ridge. Felt like walking along a knife's edge.

Turns out that was a great decision. The routes are very well marked and maintained, and the weather was great for us the whole time! With the early start and the good weather we made good time. Instead of stopping at the first hut for the day, we just stopped there for lunch and continued to the second. The track ascends through tropical forest up past the tree line, along a ridge, and then descends and returns along a river through thick valley forest.

Staying at the second hut that evening was great! Such a nice way to spend the evening when it's raining outside, and in the off season it's so convenient since you don't have to reserve spots ahead of time. My new friend Nick and I met up with another American, Dan, who was on a whirlwind one-week trip and had a car, so we all decided to do the last two sections in one day as well and high tail it to Milford Sound that evening. We camped in pouring rain that evening in the Eglinton Valley, just before heading west through the mountains to Milford Sound. The heavy rains on the mountains in the Fiordlands was like nothing I've ever seen! The rain just runs down the sides of the mountains into the valley, creating hundreds of impromptu waterfalls and making massive rushing rivers through the valley.

Unfortunately the same weather that makes the Fiordlands impressive also makes it frustrating – visibility in the sound was very low, and the high winds meant they had cancelled cruises for the day, so we headed back out all the way to Queenstown. Dan had an AirBNB room booked, Nick and I stealth camped just outside of town, to dry out our tents from the previous night's downpour.

While we were waiting our turn to go through the one-lane Homer Tunnel, we made friends with a local bird!

Forging friendships in the fires of Mt. Doom

The impromptu waterfalls that erupt all over the mountains during the rain give the impression that the mountains are crying. It's so much water!!

Sunrise in Queenstown, looking towards the Remarkables mountain range. Queenstown was a cool place, but it is definitely a resort town. Dan described it as "the city that Tony Hawk would make if he made one." It is packed with all sorts of adventure shops and guided tours and adrenaline sports.

lessons i've learned in the rain

may 9, 2015

So now I've spent a couple days hiking in the rain, and I learned something: rain jackets are the most awful thing ever. Well, actually, that award goes to rain PANTS, but the jacket takes a close second. There is almost no situation where a rain jacket will accomplish its intended goal – that is, to keep you dry. Not only does rain seep in the openings, but wearing a glorified plastic bag isn't conducive to ridding the body of sweat during activities such as…well, living.

Don't get me wrong, I would definitely be willing to put up with this if it was the only way to protect oneself from onerous precipitation. But it's not, and it confounds me why so many people put up with it – I experienced yesterday for the first time the joys of hiking with an umbrella. Yup, an umbrella.

Let me illustrate briefly: you know when it's raining outside and it's so delightful to sit inside and watch it, happy that you aren't outside in it? That's what it's like hiking with an umbrella. You get to watch the rain without having to deal with it. I've compiled a (non-extensive) list of the pros and cons for each mode of rain protection:

Rain Jacket
Doesn't keep you dry
Is miserable to hike with
Is a hassle to get out and put away
Makes you all sweaty
Only partially protects body

Umbrella
Keeps you dry
Is delightful to hike with
Takes no time at all to get out and put away
Doesn't make you sweaty
Keeps hands, face, and pack dry as well

I'll finish with a little haiku (wait…aren't all haikus the same size, by definition?)

Happy octagon,
Forcefield deflecting the rain.
Little nylon sun!

rain lessons: update

may 11, 2015

So! After today I need to update my pros/cons list for the umbrella/rain jacket debate.

Umbrella con: Easy to lose. After a number of close calls already this trip, it's finally gone for good. The man who I hitchhiked with from Lumsden to Queenstown is now one umbrella richer.

Rain Jacket+Pants pro: Indispensable for being "that weird guy standing on the bow of the ship in gale force winds and rain." No umbrella could stand up to that. And it's cold and I'm standing still, so no sweat. And it's tough for EVEN ME to forget my pants.

last minute "planning"/more days in the mountains

may 11, 2015

So for the last week and a half, I haven't made any "plans," and that's been a good thing. Instead of planning in the morning where I'm going to sleep or how I'm going to get to my next destination, I wait a bit, and something unexpected and great happens ☺ By not having plans, I'm free to say yes to anything that comes up.

The sense of community among backpackers is just great! Everyone is so self-sufficient, but always helpful, and friendly if you're willing to speak up and start a conversation. It feels like a different world that exists outside of space and time.

After the night in Queenstown, I walked into the DOC center (parks dept) to ask about conditions on the Milford and Routeburn Tracks. Apparently since the Routeburn is a point-to-point track across a mountain pass, transportation is quite a hassle, especially in the off-season. The ranger started giving me contact cards and pamphlets for transport companies and I was like… whoa. Then another lady just after me said she was heading out to the track, and did I want to come along? So we left right then, super simple! Because of a bit of a late start, I only got to the first hut, but all was good because the people coming in from the other direction were

Routeburn Track had an enormous number of these swinging bridges that swayed and twisted under you as you crossed. A bit nervous that some of them said "Max Capacity: 1 Person." Simultaneously awesome and frightening 😱

At a cool bend in the river, a triangular mountain rose up out of the elbow. With the clouds it was so surreal. The environment continues to remind me of the game "Myst." Though it's also equal parts Jurassic Park and Lord of the Rings.

23

SOAKED and COLD. I did, however, leave my pack at the hut and take a short walk further along the track and came back. Glad I did, because that way I got to see the peaks before and after they got covered with snow ☺

Anyway, had a great evening in the hut with all kinds of people by a nice fire. I spent the next few days hiking with a great Belgian couple and sheepishly practicing my French ☺

I hadn't arranged transport from the end of the track, so the Belgians helped me out with my first time hitchhiking! Got back to Te Anau to plan the next leg. While there, ran into someone I'd met while hiking Kepler, and he just raved about the Doubtful Sound cruise, so I decided to do that rather than wait and try for Milford again.

Camped at the hostel in Te Anau and got up bright and early for the cruise ☺

Looking down the valley towards Glenorchy.

View out from Harris Saddle before the snow.

More views out from Harris saddle. Couldn't get enough of this.

This one includes Harris Lake.

Harris Lake again. SOOO BEAUTIFUL!

And now for the "after" pics, with a light dusting of snow. Just…epic.

With the sun just "peaking" out 😉

Descending down into Mackensie Hut.

Yes, this is the trail. Yes, it looks like you're just walking up a creek after it rains. Waterproof boots are my friends.

miscellaneous awards

Some random thoughts:

Song of the day: "Wildflower" by MitiS

Runner up for song of the day: "Tshirt Weather" by Circa Waves (it's currently 40ish degrees and it's been raining for a week lol)

Best improvised gear award: The Belgians I met who were cycle touring needed rain gloves, but waterproof gloves are (a) never waterproof and (b) expensive. So they got a pair of those kitchen dishwashing gloves. $2 – awesome. I got myself a pair as well.

homelessness

So, I was walking along Lake Wanaka with my new friend Luke today, and I commented that in all the cities I've been in here for the last couple weeks I haven't seen a single homeless person in all of New Zealand.

Just now, though, as I was hanging around the small downtown after dark at about 7:30p with my backpack hunting for free wifi hotspots, an Asian family walked up to me and in somewhat broken English asked me if I had eaten yet tonight. I was somewhat caught off guard, and half planning to eat a second dinner soon, I said no. She then gave me a box containing most of a pizza, still warm, their leftovers from dinner.

And then I realized. I am the homeless person here. I am lowering New Zealand's beauty by being a homeless backpacker bum, lol.

Whatever, it's free pizza. Trying not to get grease on my screen as I type this. But the worst part is it's like 40°F right now and I had to take off my gloves to eat it and now my hands are numb 😊

i'm on a boat

may 13, 2015

That's right, folks, I'm king of the world, on a boat like Leo, and if you on the shore, then you sure ain't me-o.

On heavy recommendation from a friend, instead of moping and waiting around with everyone else for the weather to clear around Milford Sound, I booked an overnight cruise on Doubtful Sound. While not as famous, it's much larger and much more remote. The trip included a boat ride across Lake Manapouri (christened "Lake ManiPedi" by my sister Christi) to the the Manipouri power station and the gravel road across Wilmot Pass (only accessible by boat), a bus ride over the pass to the sound, and then an overnight cruise through the sound and all the offshoots with a stop for kayaking and swimming. It was definitely a splurge and a "touristy" thing to do but so awesome.

Of course I couldn't turn down the opportunity to swim in Doubtful Sound when given the chance, but there were only a few of us willing to brave the brisk 9.5°C water 📷

On the cruise, I met someone with a car looking for company to travel to Wanaka from Queenstown, so after the cruise I hitchhiked from Te Anau to Queenstown to meet him there. What a great experience hitchhiking is! Anyway, we took off from Queenstown and he talked about the different places he'd worked in New Zeland on his travels. He took me through one of them, Arrowtown, which was the coolest, most beautiful little old gold rush town, like Columbia in the California foothills. Here was where I got to see that New Zealand has autumn colors 🍁 But it's almost like a cruel joke…I keep getting to places and it's rainy, but people say "You just missed all the sunny weather last week!"

From there we took the mountain road route past the Crown Range, instead of the highway. Mountain roads are always better 🏔️

Wanaka is a lovely town, set next to a perfect little lake and surrounded on three sides by high mountains ranges, so they "claim" they don't get much rain. Until I got here. And then it decides to rain for four days. But there have been the most spectacular rainbows!

Māori legend has it that sometimes…in a great while…the sun appears over the Fiordlands. But the rest of the time it's busy getting its SEVEN METERS OF ANNUAL RAINFALL. That's right folks, 276 inches for those of you still not on metric.

What do ogres, onions, parfaits, and mountains have in common? They all have layers!

Before it got too cold.

We got some good vistas, despite Mother Nature's "veiled" attempt at covering up the mountains with clouds 😆

Heading out of port into Doubtful Sound. Since this place is so remote, the bus drivers and ferry captains and power plant operators spend their whole workweek living at the sound, and only cross the lake back to civilization on their weekends.

AFTER it got too cold. Notice I didn't go inside, I just put on every jacket I had. Count 'em: I've got three on at the same time lol.

I'll throw in more factoids so these mountain pics don't get repetitive: all the rain leaches tannins out of the bark of the trees and then the fresh rainwater floats on top of the salt water. The result is the top few meters of water is not salty and much darker, meaning nothing lives in the top layer, and many deep sea marine animals live much closer to the surface due to the reduced light.

Obligatory pano. Crazy to think in the past, there have been people who have made one of these small islands in the sound their home for a matter of years.

The beautiful little gold rush town of Arrowtown, showing off its fall colors.

Through the Crown Range! The van I was in had about the worst defrosters ever, so I did my duty as passenger to find the optimal combination of window venting and air conditioning to keep it clear

Gotta hand it to them. New Zealand has the best rainbows I've ever seen. I've seen double and triple rainbows, the full half circle on a lake in front of mountains.

I got just enough sun upon arriving to Wanaka to tease me ☼

on seatbelts

may 13, 2015

Well, I had my first contact with the NZ police today, and I have to say, they seem like pretty reasonable people.

Also, let me say that if you get in a car with someone you don't know, or don't know very well, not a bad idea to use a seatbelt.

My driver had a bit of a mishap while parking, and drove off the embankment. We're both alright, but we had to talk to the police and get a tow truck. I was joking with the tow truck driver that I didn't want to pay for all the expensive adrenaline adventures in Queenstown, so I just got my free one in Wanaka. Someone else asked if we parked on the side of the hill because the parking lot was full.

I found out after all this, that apparently Asian drivers are somewhat of a big problem on the NZ streets. I guess many of them have never done much driving, if any, in their home country since either big city traffic is too crazy or they come from a small rural town, and they've done just enough to get a permit or license. Also, I hear that the only travel/working visa you can get to leave China is to New Zealand. So it's easy to just fall prey to the stereotype of Asian drivers, but it's gotta be pretty difficult to transition cultures like that, and takes a lot of courage and motivation.

Aw, what a cute little tow truck 😵

roy's peak/braving the weather

may 14, 2015

So there's a dilemma that every adventurer must face at some point or another I imagine – when the weather goes south (ha! I made a pun!) do you wait it out or head out anyway?

This seems to be a common conversation topic here. I think the weather here is part of the adventure, and I'm much more likely to decide what I want to do, then only check the weather to decide how best to prepare for doing the thing, not whether or not to do it. With this approach though, it's really important to have the right gear to remain safe – it's incredible how much and how quickly the weather changes on the mountains. I didn't expect much when the mountains are only 1500m tall (5000ft), but the ranges are so geographically small and close to the ocean anything is possible.

Yesterday I took a chance on a local peak called "Roy's Peak" just outside Wanaka and close to Mt. Aspiring National Park. Hitching a ride to the trailhead a few kilometers away was much better than the otherwise hour and a half walk, but came with a warning from the local that the weather up there "wouldn't be great" (I, uh, have edited his language for sensitive ears) and that apparently a few people up there die every year and recently they lost an American girl in the area.

I think it inspired some confidence in him, however, that

Haha you say the trails are well maintained in your country? How cute! Here in NZ they HAVE LAWNS for trails. Lol.

Occasionally the clouds cleared for a moment to see some epic mountains to the southwest, but I only stopped at the top long enough to put on my thermals. No picnic lunch 😄

I had my ice axe with me, since there was some visible snow at the peak, and I had plenty of extra clothes in a dry bag in my daypack.

One thing that could have been better, though, was my shoes. I developed some pretty wicked blisters on my pinky toes the last few days from breaking in my new winter boots, and I knew my feet couldn't take another day, so I had on my trail running shoes. This proved to be a very wet and cold decision as I hiked through puddles, slush and snow. But, as I said earlier, having the right gear is awesome and I got to test the limits of my awesome wool Darn Tough socks. I can attest to the fact that they are very warm, even when soaked with icy water, and amazingly even after over a week of hard use, they don't smell AT ALL. I also brought along to New Zealand a few different styles of Darn Tough socks, but hands down the 100% wool hikers are the way to go. Seriously, get a pair. And they have a lifetime replacement policy. I also got to use my kitchen dish gloves over my regular gloves and they worked great!

Unfortunately, the weather was dreadful enough that I couldn't take many pictures, but oddly enough I still really enjoyed myself. And what's better, I saw like 6 other people out there as crazy as myself 😆

Looking out over Wanaka. Seeing the views with clouds is kind of like reading a book...you have to fill in some of the images from your imagination 🙂

escaping the funk in wanaka

may 15, 2015

No, that's not a reference to the way I smell because of not showering, though I might get a chance to do that tonight. Had a bit of a weird few days here, but feeling good after a nice day today.

I know it's silly, but I get stressed if I don't "make the most" of each day. But I need to step back and just remember whatever happens, I'm here in an amazing place, and there's another day tomorrow 🏔 With the car incident the day I got here, and the subsequent bad weather, it's been tough to get out of town. Add to that the fact that even though the weather is finally clearing today (we're having "fine spells" as I should say) I have to stay in town because I'm really having some issues with my left knee. Some things I got to do instead:

1. Help Christi with her chemistry homework from halfway across the world! 🖤
2. Read.
3. Go thrifting! Replaced my umbrella with a bomber golf-type one, and got a cheap muffin tin to make cupcakes!
4. Bake cupcakes. Gonna meet up with a friend of a friend here, and want to give them something 🎁
5. Hot yoga.

Now that the weather's cleared, I can show you which mountain is Roy's Peak:

That's Roy's Peak, overlooking the area.

more awards

may 12, 2015

Best local band: Monty Bevins (this is the guy who rode a bicycle the whole length of the island, carrying his gear and playing shows along the way) https://www.youtube.com/channel/UC6VPH9liBYtEKrzAR8kfQWA

Runner-up for best local band: A guy from Wellington who I hitched a ride from introduced me to these guys, who got their start in Dunedin – SIX60 "Don't Forget Your Roots" http://youtu.be/vqnwqsJYyiU

Best improvised gear award: using a 1.5L Smartwater bottle as a foam roller for working on my left knee.

Weirdest unknown sport: Netball. I reckon cricket is weirder, but at least I've heard of cricket. Ever heard of netball? It some weird variation of basketball.

Selfie of the day:

things around town in wanaka

may 12, 2015

So apparently lots of people come here to go four-wheeling, as I'm seeing lots of utes (that's trucks, guys) with snorkels on the intakes. The rain had made the gravel road out to Mt. Aspiring National Park pretty sketchy, with allegedly two deep-water fords. That's one reason I hung around town for the day.

A REAL adventure vehicle.

It's a LONG walk

Also, each time I walked into town I walked along this incredible tile strip. It's a timeline from year zero to year 2000, with one tile for each year. In the early years, they list notable events every few tiles, but more recently they list events every tile. Very fun and informative!

Oh, that fateful day.

Laughed a bit when I saw this – I guess "Chapter 5" means something different in the U.S., but here it apparently means buying high-end clothing at a small boutique. Ah, which perhaps then leads to the American meaning of Chapter 5. I guess it all makes sense.

A bankruptcy store??

I like to walk against them. Just to be a rebel.

Just admire that!

I am really at a loss as the point of these "barbs" when you walk into grocery stores. Are they to keep you in? Are they there to punish the people who go in but forget to grab a cart (whoops, I mean trolley) or basket? I'm skinny enough I can squeeze back through when I inevitably forget, so they fail on that account. And they don't keep you from stealing the trolleys, as they aren't at the exit. They feel like those turnstiles at sports stadiums.

And this is just TOO great of a hipster specimen. I can't believe now that I've never seen this before. This dog is not on a leash, but on a long SCARF. Right now it looks manageable, but upon walking, the scarf unfurls and looks FABULOUS. Also note: totally hipster shoes, bowler hat, and face eaters (big sunglasses…not NZ slang).

This shelf looks so…fertile.

Anyone up for pizza…and putt putt?

Ah yes. The eggs. It feels wrong. They're just…sitting there. Warm. And yet! Same shelf life as in the U.S. Oh! And on a similar note, I have NOT gotten food poisoning from the meat here even though processors here don't drench their meat in antimicrobials. Methinks the U.S. is too picky.

Leave it to the land down under the land down under to bring you wood fired pizza…in a truck…permanently located in a putt-putt golf course. Of course I tried it, but commiserated with my fellow pizza aficionado Bill Funkhouser that the crust fell short of expectations, as it often does with trucks ☹

green acres is the place to be
may 20, 2015

Introspective song of the day: "Whispers" by Passenger

Runner-up song of the day: "Living Color" by MitiS

Improvised gear FAIL Award: camp stove as toaster

So it turns out this doesn't work very well.

Let's see…where did we leave off? Ah yes, Wanaka. I had planned to go up the West Coast, but it turns out that really the best way to experience Mt. Cook (Aoraki) is from the east side. I hadn't planned on going up the center of the island, but armed with this new information I detoured to head up and meet a friend of a friend in Fairlie, whose parents owned a big farm. What a great experience to hang out on a farm for a couple days after time in the cities! My host family was so down to earth, and I got to learn a bit of local slang…every time I said "huh?" or when I would call something a certain word and they would giggle a bit. Here's a sampling of some words in context, see if you can figure them out:

1. You go swimming in your togs.
2. Instead of wearing boots or shoes, you may wear a pair of jandals to the beach.
3. When I would say something weird, they might "pay me out," or "take the piss out of me" (tease me).
4. If I need something warm to pull on before going out, I might put on a jersey.
5. After some work, you often take a smoko, regardless of whether smoking is involved. This one might be a real southern phrase though.
6. If you've got a lot of junk or dirt to move, hopefully you've got a friend with a ute.
7. If you're in a hurry and need to finish your drink quickly, you scull it.
8. If you need some cardboard for a hitchhiking sign, you can "scab" it from a dumpster behind a store or something.
9. In the afternoon you might go for a cupper, if you want a bit of tea.

I got to try the best pies in all of New Zealand, at the Fairlie Bakery. Worth the trip for a pork belly and apple pie with cracklings on top. Also, apparently what Americans refer to as bacon is here called "streaky bacon," and the more common bacon here is called middle bacon and includes more meat. Kind of like a cross between ham and bacon. Also, the fruit labeled as "feijoas" I had assumed was small guavas, as it tasted and looked just like

39

a fruit my Aunt Darlene had prepared for me and called guava. I have been informed that it is in fact a different fruit and was treated to a feijoa and ginger cake 😊

The farm I stayed at was huge! The two sons there were currently working on building a dirt road from the front of the property to the back, over a couple hills, so I got to operate a 21-ton digger. It was a blast!

Riding with the farm dogs in the back of the ATV. Hope I don't get pulled over by the farm police.

Another total surprise here is that it's common in NZ to farm deer! Venison is a common meat for export, but they also export a lot of young deer antlers to China for herbal remedies. On this farm they were raising sheep, cows, and deer, and had a pet fawn they were currently nursing. Had to take my chance feeding a fawn from a bottle! The guys also showed me a video of how the venison farming industry started, from capturing wild deer from helicopters. Helicopters would chase deer, and someone would jump from the helicopter and tackle the deer! It made cattle roping look a bit sissy. They eventually developed net guns to trap the deer with, but it still was a pretty crazy profession for quite a while.

Also got a chance to watch a CLASSIC NZ zombie movie called Black Sheep. Without spoiling the premise

"Wanna see me move twenty tons with my fingertip??"

I'll call you Bambi.

Me being a REAL man!

From the top of a silo. Rolling hills FOREVER!!

too much, I'll just say that it involves baa-aa-aa-aa-d zombies 😉 After the movie was a proper bonfire with a pile of brush and branches that needed to be burned, and we toasted some marshmallows. It was at this point that I realized I'm seeing, for the first time in my life, a brand new set of stars and constellations! For the first time I was able to see the southern cross, although I found out that I had missed out on a "fairlie" strong showing of the Aurora Australis a few nights before due to the cloud cover where I was 😣

On my last day with Louise (my new friend!) we headed over to Mt. Cook and she impressed me with her extensive knowledge of New Zealand's native flora and fauna. Apparently pine trees aren't native, so all the areas in the mountains where I feel truly at home, aren't truly NZ. And one reason many of the mountains are brushy and barren is because they've been burned many times, by the Māoris to hunt moa (the birds) or by the Europeans. New Zealand's history as a small remote island is fascinating with how many species of animals and plants have been introduced, and the Department of Conservation spends an absolutely staggering amount of effort now to control the introduced pests and hopes to return the nature to its former natural habitat.

The pyro in me is loving this.

The coolest church in NZ...or at least the one with the best view 😎 (Church of the Good Shepherd, on Lake Tekapo)

The view from said church 🙂

And I'll leave you with a sneak peek of Mt. Cook National Park. More on that later 😉

tips 4 hitchhiking
may 23, 2015

1a. Be attractive.

1b. Don't be unattractive.

1c. Sometimes pitiability works as a replacement for attractiveness, but it's a fine line. Drivers may take pity on a hitchhiker in the rain because that's a miserable situation to be in, but drivers also don't want a bunch of wet gear and people in their cars.

2. Look happy. Smiling, dancing a bit, and waving goes a long way. A lot of drivers enjoy a happy conversation partner.

3. Don't have too much baggage. (Sounds kind of like a relationship, doesn't it?) If you do, hide it until they've already stopped, then spring it on them.

4. Walk far enough out of town that you minimize local traffic.

5. Choose a highway that has one obvious destination.

6. If in a car park looking for a ride home, knock on windows and annoyingly ask everyone if they're headed back into town.

7. Be flexible.

8. This should go without saying now, but once in the car always wear a seatbelt 😆

9. Payment isn't expected, but if you've "arranged" a ride with a new acquaintance (as opposed to thumbing it on the street) it is courteous. Also, if your destinations are the same, a coffee is a nice gesture upon arrival.

10. Oddly enough, it's usually the small sedans and locals that stop, not the campervans with the tourists that you would expect to have space and be full of adventurous partying young people.

stars, mountains, and adventures

may 31, 2015

What a beautiful day at Mt. Cook Village!

Wowwee! I've had some trouble last two weeks getting Internet! But I'm ready now to unload some pixels and words on you guys.

So after my farm stay in Fairlie, weather forecast for Mt. Cook was looking up. Louise drove us out to Mt. Cook/ Aoraki and we went for a day hike, but it was windy, overcast, and a bit rainy. She went home, and I bummed around a bit until dark. There was a public shelter for hanging out and cooking that I made dinner in and went through some pictures on my phone. By about 9pm, it became clear that no one was going to come by and close it up, so I put out my bag and spent the night there ☺ Most places here in the winter go into hibernation mode, and places aren't checked or serviced. Makes stealth camping quite a bit easier. Woke up to a nice frosty morning, but there was not a cloud in the sky!

Went into the visitor center and booked a room at the Mueller hut up on the mountain. These silly temperature conversions still throw me for a loop…the DOC ranger told me that in the hut it will get below 0°, and did I have a warm enough sleeping bag for that? And I was like…ummm…how many jackets do I have that I can wear? Until I realized she meant Celsius. Which is 32°. Which is how cold I had slept in the night before, so no sweat (literally!). I knew the hike would start off with the same area I had day hiked with Louise the day before, which was about a gazillion steps, only this time with a 20kg pack. I've always wondered why trail breakers bother with switchbacks, and now I know why…flights of stairs going straight up the mountain are just silly.

Yup, this is the trail. The track up to Mueller Hut becomes very free-form…guess the only real guidance is to go "up de hill."

Taking it easy, made it halfway up the mountain (600m elevation gain) before I hit snow. And before the trail essentially turned into picking your own path scrambling up boulders with hands and feet. Then it smoothed out, but turned into a 40° incline hillside with about a foot of snow. Finally! Time for the crampons and ice axe ⊼ Watching everyone else sliding around gave me quite a serious superiority complex, but I really think it could be super dangerous hiking that face in the snow without.

I got up to the top and sighted the Mueller hut…it was quite impressive! Had lunch, but had some time to kill in the afternoon, so I headed out south, farther along the ridge.

Getting back to the hut, found a guy I'd met at the visitor center the day before, so we were like insta-friends. Guess that's kinda how it works out here – meet once, and you're an acquaintance, randomly meet again and you're insta-friends. This guy was here with his friend,

Track got pretty steep. They had us walking up like a 40° slope with no snow and no switchbacks. It was great! But I was glad for the crampons and axe ⊼

Looking back down the valley towards Mt Cook village. The rivers that flow through glacial valleys form braids and look really cool.

Looking again towards Mt. Cook

Looking towards Mt. Cook.

Situated just under the peak of Mt. Olivier, Mueller Hut is pretty spectacular! All the supplies get delivered by helicopter.

and they had actually met in Skagway, AK where she drove sled dogs and he was a mountaineering guide. After dinner, a lot of people went out to check out the stars, and they were THE BRIGHTEST STARS I'VE EVER SEEN OMG. Seriously, wish I had a DSLR, cause there'd be some awesome night photography all up there, with snow capped mountains. Which is actually the backdrop on my phone ◪ But the best was yet to

Once over the ridge, looking behind Mueller.

OH MY GOSH SO BEAUTIFUL! Sunrise over Mt. Cook. This was the most epic sunrise ever, and trust me, I took quite a few more pictures than I'm showing here. Here's a little time lapse, to show you how the colors evolved over the snow-covered alpine landscape.

From the top of Mt. Olivier

Walking along the ridge behind Mueller Hut.

Hard to believe all this is under 2000 meters (6600 ft) tall! Feels like I'm in the Himalayas! Well, except Mt. Cook, but that's the tallest in New Zealand and still only 12,000 ft.

come…sunrise over Mt. Cook was so pretty!! Lol and the best part about winter is that you don't even need to get up early to see sunrises 🌄

With my new insta-friends we headed south along the ridge again, but actually climbed a couple of the smaller summits, as it turns out he had just finished a 5-month employment as a glacier guide on the west coast.

We all then hiked down, and as he was headed back to Queenstown, he dropped me off in Cromwell on the way, after a good meal at the local pub. That night in Cromwell was certainly an experience. I must say, I have a new respect for four-season tents. I found a free camp-site/field area on the campsites app, and he dropped me there. But…it was right next to a lake, exposed with no windbreaks, on a SUPER windy and blustery night, with rock-hard ground. I took it as a challenge and learning experience to set up my awesome little tent in awful conditions, and used all of my extra stakes and rope to provide extra support to the walls. Took me about 45 mins to set up, and I tried to do it parallel to the wind so it wouldn't act like a sail. Also left both ends open so the wind could blow through. I thought I had done it, and put in earplugs so I wouldn't hear the wind howl. About an hour later, though, I felt that dreaded feeling of tent material collapsing in on me. And then…and then I sat there, outside my tent for way too long, wondering where to go, how to pack up my stuff without it all blowing away as I did it, etc. Town was about 4 km away, and it was 10:15p, so a hostel was out as well. I had arrived at night, so I didn't know if there were any buildings around as windbreaks. But I bumbled around a bit and got my stuff over to the bathroom, and sat down inside, on a very welcome (if very short) bench. And thought "this could work." And then I looked up, and realized there was no roof, except over the stall. And thought, well, I hope it doesn't rain. So I curled up on the bench. And then, about two hours later, I felt raindrops on my face. So, without letting myself realize how much of a homeless bum I'd suddenly become, I spread out my mattress and sleeping bag on the ground in the (thankfully very large and clean) stall with roof, locked the door, and slept until sunrise. And then hitched a ride to Wanaka, on the way to the west coast! I had debated taking the bus up the coast, but the bus only traveled that way every Sunday and I was not excited about the prospect of three more days in Wanaka waiting for the bus. I only stopped in to Wanaka to eat breakfast and use the Internet, and ended up hanging out with a fellow backpacker who'd had almost as crazy a night as me, but there in Wanaka. There must be dozens of us crazy folk here, dozens I say!!

With Wyatt and Hannah on top of Mt. Olivier.

One last shot of this icy, alpine wilderness 😃

the wild wild west pt. 1: if big sur and the himalayas had a baby...

june 1, 2015

From near the top of Isthmus Peak, outside Wanaka

Improvised gear award: using the cement as a can opener. Yup, that's right. One important skill I learned before leaving the states is that you can grind down the top of the can on the sidewalk and then just pop the top off. Takes about 5 mins 😎

In some ways, the west coast here is reminiscent of the foothills of the Central Valley in California. Some small gold rush towns, old mining operations, some rolling hills. But in other ways it's completely different. It rains most days of the year, and it's almost completely isolat-ed from the rest of the island – it's connected only via Haast Pass and Arthur's Pass. As you drive north along the coast, it's GREEN foothills instead of the customary "golden" (read: brown and dead) that I'm used to. But, as you look past the green foothills, and past the lush forest, you see craggy snow topped peaks, and occasionally enormous glaciers (though less and less enormous over the past few years).

After my breakfast in Wanaka, I walked out of town and waited with my thumb out for a ride out to the coast. I

A cropped shot showing the classic knife ridges so prominent in New Zealand.

Me and my new traveling partner Jonas!

had to wait longer than usual, but after about 30 mins a German guy with a surfboard in his station wagon stopped. He said he wasn't going all the way to the coast, but there was a cool hike on the way out there, and did I want to join him? Sounds great!

So we headed out there, and sure enough there's a cool hike to the top of Isthmus Peak. We made short work of it, passing a couple hunters on the way up who had bagged a giant goat.

On the way back down, he said he also wanted to drive up the coast and would I split petrol and camping costs? We could both sleep in the car. I weighed quickly the pros and cons – I had heard traffic on the West coast would be light (i.e. difficult to hitchhike), and a car to sleep in would be nice (I've heard the weather is crazy on the coast, and not looking forward to sleeping in any more bathrooms). I said yes, and decided that whatever happened would be an adventure!

The drive out over Haast Pass had us cross such charmingly named rivers as "The Trickle," "Chink Creek," and "Dismal Creek." We quickly learned that it would have been wise to fill up with petrol in Wanaka, since it was $2.31/liter in Makarora on the way out to the coast. Do the math and that's about $8.87/gal NZD...yikes! We wouldn't see it go below $2.07/liter until much further up the coast, in Hokitika.

With not much day left after the hike, we headed for a cheap campsite that was just before the pass for the night, and I made dinner under the cover of my awesome umbrella while it rained (see? Umbrellas are better). Both of us fit in the in car, and we watched a couple episodes of Game of Thrones on his laptop before going to sleep. Woke up with frost everywhere outside the car, and ice

The frost on the picnic table was sooo cool...it was like fur, standing up on end.

Sunrise over Haast Pass, burning through the fog.

Beach and beech in the same picture! Okay, so I actually don't think those are beech trees, but it would be cool if they were.

More really cool beach landscape! I'm convinced skipping stones at beaches and ponds isn't a thing here in NZ, because all of the beaches have HEAPS of perfect skipping stones. But I'm not complaining...all our beaches in the states always seemed to be picked clean.

on the inside of the car where the moisture from our breathing had condensed and frozen. As I sat outside with all my jackets on on the frosty bench while I huddled over my camp stove, I had my second pity offering of food – some hot tea from a nearby campervan.

We set off for Haast, on the coast, then continued on up to a beach. Traveling by car up the west coast was a good idea I think, because there is much less "to do" and more places to "stop and see something." Jonas and I were getting along great! At the beach we made some lunch, and really went all out! Jonas pulled out his camp stove and I pulled out my tortillas and we made burritos with eggs, peanuts, and spinach feta cheese spread...actually quite tasty!

Stopped and checked out the Fox glacier, then continued on to the Franz Josef glacier. While the Fox glacier is bigger, the Franz Josef glacier is longer, but both are just

The majestic (and honestly pretty dirty) Fox Glacier. When it recedes, the valley walls that it was supporting crumble down on top of it, making it dirty and making walking up to it dangerous.

The Franz Josef glacier! See that tiny white patch right in the middle? Now it's quite a hike to get to it, used to be right here.

Morning outside Franz Josef. What a great view to wake up to!

shadows of what they were just a few years ago. The walk up the valley to see them is accompanied by the constant drone of helicopters ferrying guided tours onto and off of the glaciers – the only way to walk on them now.

Stopping in Franz Josef for the night, we restocked at the local grocery store and made dinner on a local picnic bench, under a street light, then camped just out of town with all the campervans.

Let me briefly say that they have PERFECTED the art of the speed bump that slows you down, on the roads into the glaciers. They are speed bumps, but with cobble-stones or large river rocks haphazardly strewn into them so that it sounds like your car is going to rattle apart as you go over them. No way to cheat.

The next day took us to Okarito lagoon, out on the coast, with a spectacular panorama of rainforest, lagoon, and snowy alpine peaks.

Then on up the coast we arrived in Hokitika, which has

The Fox Glacier used to fill this whole valley! And used to fill most of it as recently as a few years ago.

Panoramic view of Okarito Lagoon, with the Southern Alps in the background.

Truly a classic west coast view. Thick jungle with craggy snowy mountains behind.

The Hokitika river gorge. Just wow. Such color.

I tried not to be boring in my pose for this picture. And just ended up being weird. Note also my careful use of complementary colors so I stand out from the color of the water.

This is right next to town?? Sign me up!

definitely got to be my favorite city on the west coast. From the map, I didn't expect it to be anything special, but it is the largest city between Haast and Greymouth, and has enough flatland between it and the mountains that you can drive for 30 mins through the "countryside," complete with farmland and families out riding bikes and stuff, until you arrive at the river gorge. Which is SPECTACULARLY beautiful. Hokitika is also the best place in NZ to buy jade carvings and jewelry (pounamu).

the wild wild west pt. 2: if big sur and the amazon had a baby...

june 2, 2015

I guess Jonas and I really are friends, because I got to drive us today! Am happy that I finally got to drive on the "wrong" side of the road 🚗

We drove up through Greymouth, the biggest city on the west coast, and on up to Punakaiki to see the "pancake rocks." All the talk of pancakes was making us hungry, and we wanted desperately to make some pancakes. But the weather wouldn't cooperate to give us a break in the rain long enough to bust out the stove. Bummer.

The drive from Greymouth to Westport was the most striking coastline I've seen, definitely worth the drive. It definitely is rainforest, but the craggy coastline that contains it is remarkeable.

Before leaving civilization behind in Westport to venture out into the remote Kahurangi National Park, we stopped at the local swimming/sports complex and did a swim workout and took nice long hot showers. No one made a fuss about us swimming in our underwear (do they call them knickers here? Pants? Trousers? Still trying to figure this one out.) I have to say though, this

Heavily forested beaches!

was the first day here that I've really gotten frustrated. In general, the hut system for backpacking in NZ is great, but we spent about an hour hassling around trying to book a spot in the huts in the Heaphy Track. Unlike the other great walks, this one wasn't "off season" – it's year round so full price even in winter. And in Westport the DOC office keeps weird hours so we couldn't talk to

Everyone kept talking about the pancake rocks, but I had no idea what to expect...or what made them "pancake-y." Pretty cool.

56

More pancakes.

them. We sat in the car for about an hour, on Jonas's cell phone, registering for online accounts with the DOC, filling out an itinerary, trying to pay by Visa, only to find out that they use the "Verified by Visa" system, so then we had to go make new accounts with Visa, after which we had to go through filling out our itineraries with the DOC again…etc etc. All to spend a couple of nights in a hut in the mountains. Maybe I was just hangry. But the other huts have been MUCH easier.

Last stop on the west coast was to be Karamea – the start of the Heaphy Track, and also home of the Oparara Arches.

Plenty of regular rocks along the beaches too!

I didn't feel like they could be adequately described by only one picture, because I'm not good enough at taking pictures.

the wild wild west pt. 3: "300" edition

may 12, 2015

New Zealand: "Our rainforests…will blot out the sun!"

Me and my Spartan hiker mates: "Then we will hike in the shade."

Seriously, the rainforest near the beaches in the Kahu-rangi National Park was untamed jungle status, and I couldn't imagine hiking through it without an established track. The Heaphy track is a 78 km point-to-point hike, and the two ends are separated by almost 500 km of road. To manage the task of transportation, it was my idea to park at the beginning, hike most of the way to the end, turn around and hike back. To avoid paying a ridiculous amount of money in hut fees, though, this would mean an awful lot of hiking each day, since normally either direction takes 4 days. My itinerary would include 22.8 mi the first day (with packs), 28 mi the second day (without packs), and then 22.8 mi the last day (again with packs). The first day was definitely a long day…I think Jonas wasn't quite ready for it. Guess this'll be good training for a thru hike 🧦

The walk in was pretty awesome! It definitely had the feel of walking along a beach on a remote Pacific Island. It was dense jungle, packed with palm trees and vines. And yes, turns out it IS possible to swing on vines 🌴

As we got higher up, the weather turned colder and wetter, and we were met with ferocious bouts of hail. With a layer of slushy snow and plenty of water and mud, once again I failed the test of proper footwear choice in my quest to get used to hiking in my trail runners. But my

Some seriously thick jungle status all up in here!

Todd, Chris, Kate, and Jonas, at the Heaphy Hut

58

The hail fell thick enough to cover the ground like coarse snow. And the picture here doesn't convey the extent of the bootsucking (or tennis-shoe-sucking) mud present while they performed trail maintenance.

There's a pole between Gouland Downs and the ridge where hikers past have hung up their old, worn out boots. This isn't the only place here I've seen this...wonder if it's a kiwi thing?

There were a few of these signs along the trail warning us about the carnivorous snails, and they made me think of my mom. She LOVES snails. Though I haven't been able to figure out if they were warning us to be careful of the snails, or be afraid of the snails.

Heaphy Track simultaneously earns the prizes in my book for best huts, and dodgiest bridges.

shoes and socks once again came out like champs!

Jonas was fading towards the end, but he asked to borrow my trekking poles, and fell in love with them…I haven't been able to get them back! After that point I struggled to keep up with him 🚶

That evening though, he said…"uh oh…I think I didn't bring enough food"…

I asked him how much had he brought? He had a few wheetabix, some raisins, two carrots, and a chocolate bar. For two more days of food with almost 25 miles each day. Lol, looks like we're gonna be sharing food 😵

Next day was really tough for me (I think because it was so chilly), but Jonas was FLYING with my trekking poles, couldn't stop talking about how he wanted to buy a pair in Nelson. We didn't get quite to the top of the ridge because we were in danger of racing daylight to get back. But we still clocked about 25 miles the second day. With all the mud the first day, my pants had gotten filthy, and I had been looking with jealousy at my friends' gaiters, which I had thought were really only useful in snow. This day though, I used mine with my boots and simultaneously found out how cool gaiters are for muddy hiking and creek crossings, and why stiff boots aren't the typical choice for 25 mi days 😄 Got some fun blisters to keep me company for the last day.

The weather for the last day was perfect – I don't know how we've been so lucky to have cloudless weather for 5 out of our 6 days on the coast!

When we got back to the car, with all my food exhausted, Jonas whipped up quite the gourmet meal, involving

I have to imagine my mother would have had a hard time walking across these bridges…but i thought they were pretty fun 😊

both of his camp stoves and mine, with a soup and a main course and all sorts of veggies. Delicious!

We went to sleep with the promise of pancakes in the morning, which were delicious as well, btw 😊

My official recommendation for Kahurangi National Park is to start from Kohaihai (near Karamea) and either day hike into Heaphy Hut or, if you want to experience more swing bridges, continue on to Lewis Hut for the night. That's the best, most unique scenery. Then, on the

Beautiful weather, and oh so tropical!

This river was creatively named "Big River."

way out, drive in to the Oparara Valley (14 km dirt road) to see some spectacular natural rock features and rainforest. It's pretty wild the color of the water here – the rivers are the color of black tea, but clear – not muddy, presumably from the dyes they leach out of the tree bark.

This is the Oparara Arches. It was really difficult to get a picture of this!

the food post

june 2, 2015

Improvised gear award: Using my bandana as an insulating pot cozy. By adding this, I really have recreated my JetBoil in functionality, at a fraction of the weight. And I can take off the pot handles!

In a lot of ways, the food here in New Zealand is a backpacker's paradise. A few examples:

1. On the nutritional panel, most foods have a column next to "amount per serving" that is labeled "amount per 100g," giving the nutritional breakdown per standardized 100g portion, in addition to the breakdown per whatever arbitrary portion size they've assigned. This aids immensely in choosing both calorie-dense food and food with a high calories per dollar ratio.

2. The cereal aisles are SPECTACULAR! Whereas American stores are filled with uncountable varieties of "puffed" and sugary cereals for kids, the stores here instead have the whole aisle full of different varieties of muesli, which is much more dense and nutritious. I am in love with muesli 🖤

3. In the states, I have only ever been able to find powdered SKIM milk (called "trim" milk here), but here you can buy powdered WHOLE milk. I love it!

I'm also enjoying this as a sort of learning experience on how to cook for myself entirely from nonperishable food. I've kind of gotten into the following routine:

In the morning, two cups water with some powdered whole milk, and about half a bag of muesli. Heat it up if there's frost on the ground ❄ Total about 1500 cals, $3.

While hiking, granola bar every hour or so. Then for lunch, a tortilla with Nutella and peanut butter and either dried whole bananas or banana chips. I've never been a Nutella person before, but for some reason now I can't get enough of the chocolate + banana thing. Total maybe 800-1200 calories, $5.

For dinner, I boil two cups of water, turn off the stove and add about a cup of cous cous, a meal/sauce flavoring packet, and about two tablespoons of oil. In about 3 mins I've got an awesome dinner that actually tastes like the meal the seasoning packet says it is. These packets come in like 50 different varieties at the grocery store and are

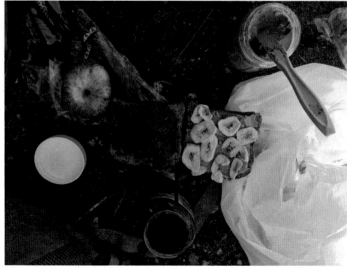

This may not look like much, but boy is it delicious. Kicks the pants offa PB&J!

like a $1.50, so it's pretty cool. If I'm in town I can grab a fresh vegetable and add that. Cous cous is like my new best friend! I was really into instant rice in the states, but I can't find that here, and a bike touring couple turned me on to cous cous. Total maybe 800 calories, $3.

I got a cheap Chinese titanium backpacking stove from a company called Olicamp before I left the states, as an experiment. I didn't expect it to hold up, but it's been great! Weighs one ounce, and after I took the handle off my pot and replaced it with the bandana, my whole cookset is down to like 4 or 5 oz, instead of the 14 oz with the JetBoil, seemingly without much loss in cooking efficiency. I recommend the cooking equipment from the guys over at Olicamp!

Bread is kind of a luxury item, but I've been enjoying a brand here called Bürgen, and I can just buy a loaf and eat the whole thing plain it's so delicious. I've definitely heard stories of thru hikers losing lots of weight, and I certainly hope that's true, cause I'm definitely not losing any weight here, lol. Jonas and I were bad influences on each other, and a few times we would get a bag of cookies or trail mix and finish off the whole thing while watching an episode of Game of Thrones on his phone.

Cooking up some cous cous while looking out over Haast Pass, while it rains lightly on me ☕

ah yes! Eating a mixture of banana chips and raspberry jam with a spoon! Guess this is what happens when you're short on food and scraping the bottom of the barrel 😆

And here is quite a spectacle! BOTH of Jonas's stoves, plus my backpacking stove, were commissioned to make this multi-course meal.

Jonas is real big on cooking LUNCH! Which I don't understand. Here he is roasting peanuts to add to his eggs to make some burritos.

return to civilation in nelson

june 3, 2015

Some really cool tidal plains at Abel Tasman.

After spending time in the Kahurangi NP, we headed east to complete the circuit of the island in Nelson. But! Not without a side trip to Abel Tasman National Park. AT seems to be the park with the most domestic kiwi traffic, which I guess makes sense since it's so close the populous North Island, and the country's capital of Wellington.

AT is right on the coast, is home to a lot of beaches, and apparently has a HUGE tidal variation of up to 6m. This exposes huge tidal plains at low tide, which is pretty cool. After seeing coast and forest in Kahurangi on the Heaphy Track, we just did a quick day walk and continued on to Nelson.

Another view of the huge tidal plains.

Another attempt at an interesting perspective. Maybe a good lock screen for an iPhone?

I looked and looked for a "unique" picture to take of the beach, and finally settled on this weird juxtaposition...frost on the sand, in the afternoon!

65

However, we did suffer a slight delay. I'm not sure if there's a term for the OPPOSITE of a kleptomaniac, but I'm pretty sure if there is one, it would describe me perfectly. Instead of the compulsion to take things from wherever I am, I must feel the compulsion to LEAVE things wherever I stay. I think I've left a steady trail of items all across New Zealand. I'll just think of it as "my legacy," or maybe a breadcrumb trail in case I get lost.

In this case it was my trekking poles. Jonas and I had stopped in to Motueka on our way from AT to Nelson, so he could buy a pair…at which point I realized I hadn't ever put mine in the car. Jonas was gracious enough to drive back (30 mins) and we found them propped up next to the bathroom, where I'd left them.

Looking towards the mountains of Nelson and Picton from AT.

Nelson was a really cool city! I can definitely call it a city instead of a town. It was a shock when we got in, because suddenly, for the first time in 3 weeks, I saw traffic lights! And a 4-lane road! I was driving, and I got a bit nervous. It's easy enough to simply stay on the left side of the road, but navigating around city traffic with stop lights and such requires a bit more thought 😬

There are two big car parks right in the center of town, and they're free to park in overnight, which automatically means come nightfall, the only cars left are station wagons and campervans. You know, the cars big enough to sleep in 🚐 The next morning, on Saturday, we walked over to the weekly open-air market and tried some awesome food trucks and checked out all the cool vendors before heading out for a day hike in the mountains.

And one last pic from AT. Who can tell me what's wrong with this photo? Hint: I've "left" it to you to figure it out. It'll "drive" you crazy. (steering wheel's on the "wrong" side!)

The geographical center of NZ. Good thing the north island isn't any longer, or this would be in the ocean 😆

In the evening we found the local swimming pool, went for a 30 min workout, and soaked in the hot tub before a quick shower to get ready for a "night on the town." Unfortunately, downtown seemed to be pretty deserted, even at 10:30p, so we played a couple games of free billiards before heading to bed.

Just…so pretty. Nelson is nestled up against the Richmond Range of mountains.

One of the sights around town: these guys are the ones who made "the rings" for the Lord of the Rings movies. Unfortunately they were closed when we got there, so we couldn't see "the precious."

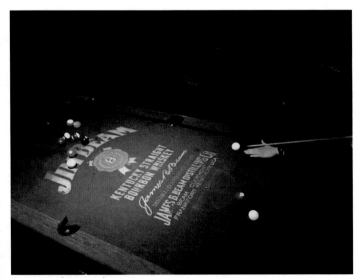

Free pool? Yes please!

Here's how cool Nelson is…there's just a random piano outside the museum for people to play.

67

goodbye south island!

june 7, 2015

I went out on deck on the ferry to get some fresh air…and noticed a familiar odor. We had some cows along for the ride!

What a wild and unexpected last couple of days! Finally said goodbye to Jonas, my travel partner of 10 days, and hopped onto the ferry to Wellington.

Onboard the ferry. This has gotta be the biggest Phillips-head screw I've ever seen!

When I arrived in Wellington, I got there just in time to walk to a nearby church, of the same branch I'd gone to in Dunedin and enjoyed greatly. Ferry arrived in at 5:30p, church was a 30-min walk right down the coolest street in town (Cuba St) and it started at 6p…perfect!! A great service, and the people invited me to the "after party" for some cards and music and junk food. Made friends and found a couch to crash on for the night. The streets in Wellington are crazy! They are without a doubt the twist-iest, narrowest streets ever, with tight hairpins all over the place, and you can only get the full experience navigating them by being driven around by a local, at night. It's like a roller coaster!

Next day, got some tips on walking places in Wellington,

Nighttime skyline of Wellington. Hands down best city so far.

Mt. Victoria - what a cool view of the city, and this hill is IN the city!

and explored Mt. Victoria (a five-min walk from the doorstep, with lots of mountain bike trails!), checked out the awesome (free!) natural science museum in downtown, called Te Papa, and then took a bus out to the shore, and walked about two hours along the coastline to an awesome beach campsite. In the morning I hitched a ride back into town and caught a bus to Tongariro.

Te Papa is one of the best natural science museums I've been to. They had a spectacular exhibit on NZ's involvement with the battle at Gallipolli.

I had also made a friend at the church party who lived in Hamilton, up north, and he invited me to stop in on my way up. I quickly made my week's itinerary and told him I'd be there Friday. I'm always nervous planning that far ahead, but I understand people's schedules aren't as flexible as a traveler's ☺

The Tongariro alpine crossing has been top of my list for the north island, and everyone raves about it. Apparently it's ranked one of the top 10-day hikes in the world (though I'm not sure by whom…) The drive north took us past spectacular coastline and gorgeous countryside.

However, in my haste to tentatively plan my week, I had not checked the weather forecast (I've gotten too used to good weather I guess), and the weather driving north got worse…and worse…and worse. We had a bus delay in Turangi, and I was chatting with the driver. He told me all about the weather forecast for the crossing, wind up to 100km/h, 30mm precip, and windchill of -6˚C. Ugh.

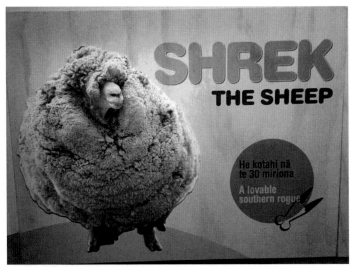

This was one of my favorite exhibits, though. A sheep that escaped shearing for six years gained national popularity and was nicknamed "Shrek."

Oh Wellington, you so silly ☺

This building of parliament in Wellington is affectionately known as "the beehive."

Ha! It's good to see NZ can laugh at themselves, and embrace the LOTR culture 😀

Tons of Māori culture here, totally different from the South Island where there's none.

Driving into the park, I KNEW there were mountains in there somewhere, but I couldn't see them through the rain and thick clouds.

I spent that evening at the hostel replanning, and hemming and hawing with a fellow not-weather-checker over the decision to hike or not. She had only 4 days left in the country, I had the luxury of 9 more days. As we talked and talked, it started thundering…enough to shake the hostel like an earthquake. She resolved to do it anyway, but I made plans to head up to Rotorua and soak in the hot springs while waiting out the rain. In all this, I saw the forecast showed the best chance at a clear day at Tongariro would be…any guesses? Yup, Friday. When I would be in Hamilton. Oh well, guess I'll have good

weather there and try for another clear day at Tongariro after that.

The bus to Rotorua didn't leave the park until 1:20p, which is longer than I wanted to wait, so next morning I struck out with my thumb out. This proved to be my most difficult hitchhike yet, with a 30 min wait in Ohakune and a 45 min wait at the turnoff to Rotarua from Taupo, and a total of 5 different cars. But I made it!

I had no idea what to expect from Rotorua, other than there were some hot springs. Turns out it's a city entirely situated in a caldera, or a kind of dead volcano crater. So there's tons of heat underneath the whole city, which means the whole region is full of hot springs, and boiling

Leaving Wellington, on my way to Tongariro. Before the weather got bad.

Even the streams feeding the lake are steaming!

And here we have steam leaking up through the brickwork.

And here in the park in the middle of town, hot pools and hot bubbling mud pits.

mud pits and steam leaking from the ground. Even walking through parts of town, there's steam leaking up out of people's yards, and boiling water gurgling out between bricks. The whole city smells like sulfur, which is causing me to constantly ask myself if I just farted. Makes me really self-conscious! Also, it's a really big place for experiencing Moari culture, which I totally didn't expect.

Something else I didn't expect, though, is that it seems as though you have to pay quite a bit to see anything. All the hot mud pools and the sulfur springs and geysers seem to be privately held, and seeing the Māori dances and shows is quite expensive. There are a few smaller hot springs and less popular attractions, but they were quite a ways out of town.

It's certainly been a bit of a struggle on this trip, deciding what to spend money on. Everything is very easy to do, if you're willing to pay for it. Many tourist attractions are way overpriced, but at the same time you can't be so tightfisted that you don't experience the very things you came here to experience. With Rotorua being the hub that it is of Māori culture and me nearing the end of the trip, I decided after much deliberation that I would splurge on my second expensive tourist attraction and cross three things off my list at once: I found an evening show at one of the local geysers (Te Puia) that included a Māori cultural ceremony (got to see and take part in a haka!), an all-you-can-eat hangi buffet (traditional Māori

pit BBQ), and a nighttime viewing of the geyser. I decided it was worth it to cough up the $105, and why wait til the next day? So I went online to book it for that night, only to find out it was too close to the showing time to book online. On a whim, I started walking. I knew it would take me 40 mins to walk there, and the show started in an hour, so I resolved to just see what would happen. When I showed up and asked if I could still get a ticket for the evening, the lady said yes, and she seemed amazed that I had walked all the way from town at night in the rain for the show, so for some reason she gave it to me for $65. And then she didn't want me walking back

A typical Māori "meeting house."

into town at 9p, so she got me a spot on the shuttle back into town for free 💰

I had thought of trying to find a camp spot near a hot beach spring, but it was a very long ways out of town and the reviews online didn't make it sound very nice. So the shuttle driver dropped me off at a backpacker's downtown that was supremely awesome…$20 beds, free rice and pasta, and free wifi! Sold.

Here's a traditional "haka." Lots of cool dancing, and we got to participate too!

Removing the hangi from the pit so we can chow down!

on to the land of steamy goodness...

june 7, 2015

So, while my INITIAL impression of Rotorua was that everything costs money, as with anything a little investigation and ingenuity goes a long ways. All around NZ, in every town and city, are "i-Sites" where you can get information on activities, tourist attractions, etc. In many towns near parks, you can also find DOC (Dept of Conservation) visitor centers. My preference is always to talk to the DOC centers, as they are staffed by outdoorsy people, while the i-Sites are staffed by random people ostensibly getting a commission to sell you tickets and bookings to tourist attractions.

The i-Site in Rotorua didn't mention the awesome day walks in town at "The Redwoods," nor the (somewhat) secret free hot pools at Kerosene Creek, 25km out of town. The backpacker's I stayed in was the coolest one I've been to so far, and offered to hang onto my bag for the day while I went out exploring. I highly recommend the Rotorua Downtown Backpacker's 👍

The Redwoods was awesome! A short hike through redwood forests brings you to the top of the ridge overlooking the entire geothermal valley (that you normally have to pay admission to actually go into and see), and takes you past numerous downhill mountain bikes trails and a very cool MTB park.

Afterwards, the goal was to get to Kerosene Creek for some hidden hot pool fun. Bit of a challenge, however, as it is 25km out of town, and Rotorua (not sure if it's

Couldn't help taking a pic of this. These are the most thorough instructions for restroom use I've ever seen!

Turquoise spring water with palm trees and redwoods in the same view. New Zealand sure is the land of unique juxtapositions!

View of the geothermal valley…see all that steam? Smells delicious 😖

On the other side of the ridge from the geothermal valley. So many trees!

just here, or north island in general) did not seem very hospitable to hitchhiking. As I walked out of town, I passed some friends from the backpacker's who had been waiting for an hour to get picked up for a ride south to Taupo, a pretty popular destination. This didn't give me much hope, as I had to get out to the springs and back in time for my bus to Hamilton at 6 pm. Given the difficult hitching, I guess choosing to take the bus to Hamilton was a good choice. Sticking with it for 30 mins, I hitched a ride to the turnoff for the springs, and walking the remaining distance down the side road in I wasn't disappointed.

Kerosene Creek, as one would expect, is an assault on the olfactory senses. Not in the typical sulfurous way, but it really does give the impression of the odor of kerosene. It was an incredibly unique spring in that there was enough geothermally heated water to heat an entire flowing creek! Only to about maybe 85°F, but it was such a treat with a light drizzle falling around. There are multiple

On the walk into Kerosene Creek, you can see the steam over even the regular lakes.

74

pools that are fed by waterfalls, but bathers are warned not to submerge their heads as amœbic meningitis can apparently be contracted if the amœbas make their way up your nose.

I did cut my stay short to guarantee my return timeline, and had just as much difficulty getting back into town, but made it with enough time to spare, eating some some dinner before hopping onto the bus. I had made a friend at church in Wellington who lives up in Hamilton who was excited to have me come stay at his awesome new house, meet his wife, and see his pet birds 😃

My uncle Steve loved finding "bubble baths" in nature. He would've loved this one, which is HEATED!!

This is a REAL hot spring.

on top of the world!

may 12, 2015

From the top of Mt. Karioi, looking out over the small surf town of Raglan.

Friday was Josh's day off (the guy I was visiting in Hamilton), so we planned to head out to the small hippie surf town of Raglan and climb his favorite mountain, Mt. Karioi. What a treat! Josh was fond of saying that Hamilton was a poor place to visit, but a great place to live. Historically known for its agriculture, there isn't much to do or see in town, but it is very close to cool places in all directions.

Mt. Karioi is a truly unique climb, starting from incredibly steep grass paddocks leading into bush, and winding up through mud and jungle and rocks. Hands are very much involved in the climb, and the scenery changes with maybe every 100m climbed. Josh was in his element here, stepping quickly around the slippery roots and mud bogs, but I made contact between my bum and the ground more than once, and was the first to plunge ankle deep in mud.

From the top it was so peaceful, looking out across the Tasman Sea, admiring the waves breaking across the shores that make Raglan the amazing surf spot that it is. We explored some new food combinations that only hikers will appreciate, such as BBQ rice crackers with soft cheese, and gradually adding peanut butter and Nutella to the mix.

By the way down I had gained a better understanding of the muddy slippery floor and stayed upright (almost) the whole time, and we got back in just enough time to get some amazing frozen yogurt in town and check out a small curio shop. The frozen yogurt was no joke! They scooped frozen yogurt into a machine that looks like a masticating juicer, added frozen fruit of your choice, and extruded it into a cone.

That night....oooh...that night I had the pleasure of

Mmm...frozen yogurt after a hot winter day 🍦

Gotta love how straightforward the kiwis are. The two popular types of cheddar cheese are "mild" and "tasty."

The drive out to Coromandel was unreal!

I'm so excited to be baking!! In an actual kitchen!!

Green spots on the map are always the best. This is where the previous picture was from. With that in mind, think how awesome the Coromandel peninsula will be (that big fat green thing at the top!)

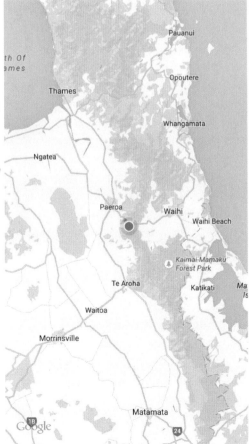

But unfortunately my social media training is not yet complete. I often forget to take a picture of the meal before it's mostly demolished. This was some shakshouka and savory muffins, with a nice light salad and homemade raspberry vinaigrette.

cooking, in a real kitchen, with nice cookware and a stocked pantry, a dinner for three! They went out to a church event and I stayed in and cooked. I was a little nervous that my skills were rusty, but it all turned out, and it was ready on time! Thanks to my sister for helping me out a bit from across the world 😎

Still waiting for a break in the weather for Tongariro, so I'm headed up to the hot water beaches on the Coromandel peninsula to dig myself a nice hot bath in the sand ⛺

my battle with tongariro. or, how i got slapped by the mountain. or, why i'm glad the forecast was wrong.

june 9, 2015

Okay, I'm going to skip talking about the Hot Water Beaches for now. But I'll get back to that later. This story has no pictures, unfortunately, but don't worry as I've made up for it by increasing the number of words 😉

There's a common frustration here with weather and hiking advice. Given the glut of tourists who are woefully unprepared for hiking in areas that are prone to rapid weather changes, the Department of Conservation rangers give very conservative advice as to whether the conditions on any given track are "safe." And perhaps they've tired of rescuing stranded hikers via helicopter, or having bad press of hikers dying. And I suppose there's nothing wrong with that, as it's only advice and they don't actually STOP anyone from heading out on the trails, but it makes it difficult to assess the situation if you are prepared for some weather.

With winter setting in, Tongariro is now off-season and in order to book a shuttle to and from the track, you have to pay for a guide, who checks the weather and furnishes you with all appropriate mountaineering gear before leading you along the track.

Everyone I've talked to picks the alpine crossing of Tongariro as the best thing to do in the North Island. And many of the people here have already done it once, but are trying to squeeze in another crossing before they leave the country.

With all this in mind, and knowing that I had all my own mountaineering gear. I decided to be a little creative and go for it myself. My bus goes right past the access road to the track, so I asked (politely!) if they would drop me off at the access road, which they did. My schedule would be really tight – I really wanted to take a trip north of Auckland still too, but with only 4 days left in the country, I would have to do the hike and get back up to Auckland in the same day, a tall order since the hike is 6-8 hours and the drive is 4.5 hours, and I've had bad luck hitching up here.

At this point in the season, weather on the mountain is generally bad, so the best you get is a good day occasionally. But the kicker is that you only get a tip from the weather service about a clear day maybe two days in advance, and without a car getting there can take both of those days just in traveling. I had missed the Friday window, but forecast said Monday would be good. Tuesday would be windy, but dry and few clouds. The soonest I could get there was Monday evening, and by cleverly getting dropped off at the access road and spending the night at the backcountry hut I could get started at daybreak and hopefully catch the tail end of the clear weather window on Tuesday.

Fortunately I did get to see on Monday evening the mountains I would be walking up, because that's the last I would see of them. I woke up before sunrise on Tuesday, very hopeful. It was very foggy outside, but that'll burn off, I thought to myself, and it's not cold. As was now my custom, I started off simply in my regular clothes, reserving my dreaded rain suit until conditions warranted. About an hour and half in, I met a couple of guys coming towards me. That's weird, I thought – it's unusual to hike the opposite direction, and far too early if they were. They were pretty well soaked, and told me I might want to put on my rain clothes sooner rather than later. I said okay, but knew I wouldn't, because rain suits are stupid. They said they had attempted the crossing, but were turning back because at the top the wind was way too strong. They had started at 5am (2 hours before me) with the same hope of beating the weather. I thought to myself that maybe they hadn't seen in the forecast that the weather was supposed to ease around midday, and I held out hope.

About 15 mins later, and a couple hundred feet higher, I noticed my fleece, though I hadn't realized it, was quite wet. The fog had turned to a thick drizzly windy mist, not so wet that you ever feel like it's raining, but thick enough that by the time you realize it, your clothes are soaked. So I stopped, put on thermals and rain suit, and carried on.

And then the wind started in earnest. As I proceeded

higher, the wind became more incessant, and the moisture it carried more stinging, such that I had to hold my hood out to block the wind from my face. Fortunately though, most of the time the wind was at my back so it was easy to ignore it.

Then I got to the South Crater. Now, I definitely couldn't SEE the crater I was in, but it was a (presumably) wide flat expanse as I no longer was climbing along the rocks. Instead, now I was walking on an icy and muddy plateau, at each trail marker pausing briefly to scan for the next marker, only 20m away but difficult to see. On the other side of the crater, the trail started climbing again, with a chain and then a cable bolted along the trail to assist hikers in the slippery and windy conditions (guess that means the weather is like this often, huh?)

If the South Crater was at all shielded from the wind, the ridge I was now on leading to the Red Crater was not shielded at all. As I got to the top of the ridge, I came to some breaks in the rocks on my right (facing east) and could see that I was now walking along a saddle. I could see the wind and mist sweeping up the crater wall to my left where I'd just walked up, and over the saddle before dropping off sharply to my right. The first of these gaps in shelter I braced for and walked across, hunching down to be less surface area for the wind, and leaning heavily into my trekking poles. The relief given by the next wall of rocks on my right was short-lived, but before the next gap I paused as the wind gusted just before I stepped out. So I've determined that my body is not a calibrated anemometer, and consequently I can't say what the wind speed was. But I imagine it must have been higher than 80km/h. The forecast told me it would be less than 50km/h.

Watching the mist blow up and over the saddle was mesmerizing! But after standing there for 5 minutes or so, I realized I had to actually decide to either keep going forward or to turn around. And then I did it. I turned around and started walking back.

Now, I'm all for hiking in bad weather, but my visibility was zero so there wasn't much scenery to admire, and I really was worried I was gonna get blown over the ridge by a sudden gust. And if it was going to clear up, it would have by now. So, I did all I could do and became a bad weather prophet to all those I passed on the way down, just as the two men had been to me. Going back was quite a bit less comfortable, as the wind was now in my face. About halfway across the South Crater (which came to be known later as "the plateau of death" by me and the people I commiserated with back at the bottom) I had to stow my glasses and continue blind, although ironically less blind than with them on, as they were covered in rain and I possessed nothing dry with which to wipe them. I passed a number of groups on their way up, many of them in JEANS, and a few in TSHIRTS.

I got a ride back into town, and since I'd finished early, I was able to catch the bus back to Auckland so I could spend my last day traveling the northern tip of the island. I also quickly checked the weather report for the mountain I was just on, and they still claimed that the weather was dry, with wind at 50km/h.

So why am I glad the weather forecast was wrong? Because I think bad experiences are just as important as good experiences. I think it's good to know what the worst case can be, so that you can judge situations better in the future. I think it was a very humbling experience for me to have to turn around, to know that I can't always brute force my way through planning, assuming that I can handle whatever comes my way. There will always be things I can't handle, things out of my control. It's good to learn to be able to say no sometimes. It's good to be uncomfortable occasionally, to remind me that I'm a small person in a huge world. To teach me not to underestimate the crazy and often dangerous world of alpine conditions. And last, but maybe not least, it gives me one more thing to come back here for.

Am I glad that I found out for myself up on the ridge that it was impassable rather than believe the first two guys I met? Definitely.

i get myself into some hot water...

june 10, 2015

Sunset on the river mouth leading to Hot Water Beach. So peaceful 🙂

One thing I was really excited to check out was the Hot Water Beach. It's a fabled beach where you can grab a shovel, dig a hole on the beach, and relax in your own personal hot tub on the beach as it fills with hot geothermal water. I was advised to go at low tide, so I checked the tide tables and determined this would be about 2:30p. My bus didn't get in until 4:40p, so I knew I'd be camping and catching it the next day, hopefully then catching the bus again back out.

Sunrise on the trail leading to the beach. So spectacular, I couldn't resist stopping for a pic.

However, I learned something new that day. Apparently the tides change by an hour every day? Did you guys know that? I thought the tides were like daylight, getting a few minutes later every night. Nope, an hour a day. And the date I had checked was two days before the day I'd get to dig, which meant low tide was at 4:30p, and I'd miss the bus back. Now I REALLY didn't want to spend another day here, even with as beautiful as the Coromandel Peninsula had turned out to be, because I still had lots to do on the North Island in my last few days. But, the extra time meant I could walk up the road to Cathedral Cove, another recommended sight.

I got to the beach about two hours before low tide, and didn't bother "hiring a spade" because I thought that was a waste of money. After all, I've dug heaps of holes (lol! Heaps of holes! Is that a pun, or an oxymoron?) on the beach with just my hands. This was a good call.

When I got there, there were a few people digging, and an extra shovel. There was a kiwi there leading the charge, and he really seemed to know what he was doing. Apparently he "lives" at the beach and just hangs out, digging a spa for himself every other day for exercise, so he knew where the best spot was and had it down to a science. After about an hour of digging we climbed in, and watched all the late comers "prospect" for hot water, as he kind of chuckled to himself and offered some helpful/slightly sarcastic advice to them. The water was so hot in the center of the pool it would burn you, so we all just sat around the edge, and soaked for about an hour.

I made friends with a group of French people, practiced

Tried out a new tent for this trip, that sets up with just my trekking poles. This is the first time I've gotten to take a picture of it set up, because I always set it up and take it down in darkness with the winter days being so short.

Since I had to wait for low tide to experience the Hot Water Beach, I walked the 6km over to Cathedral Cove. Pretty neat, but it's a one-trick pony. Just a big arch on the beach...not really worth my 3 hours walking, lol. The hole in the rock is bigger than it looks from a distance, though!

Talk about a bathroom with a view...this is the only pit toilet I've ever used that had a picture window overlooking the beach!

Here we are, madly shoveling to put up a wall before the next big wave comes in. We had a pool digging expert there to help us and organize the effort

Our pool all dug, enjoying the fruits of our labor. You can see the late comers attempting to put together another next to ours.

my French, and it turned out they were heading to Auckland that evening, which was perfect! They offered me a ride 🚗

This set me up perfectly to head out to my last two adventures, as Auckland is a bus hub.

13 tips for hosteling

june 10, 2015

Yeah, so this isn't a nice even number of tips, but it's what I could come up with, so deal with it lol. I'm getting to the last day here in NZ, so I've got a few summary lists hanging out on my phone to publish over the next coupla days.

Now, without further ado:

1. Sometimes there are "web only" discounts, especially in the city. Check online before arriving.

2. BBH hostels are more common here than YHA hostels. A really good index for finding a hostel when you get into town is bbh.co.nz

3. Free wifi is an uncommon luxury, but YHAs are more likely to have it than BBHs. I'd say it's appropriate right now for me to say my occupation is "professional wifi finder."

4. Sometimes you don't have control over the thermostat…be prepared for it to be way too hot. Protip: sleeping on your side gives your body more surface area with which to dissipate body heat.

5. In shared rooms, usually somebody snores. Bring earplugs.

6. On a similar note, the only way to avoid being woken up by someone else's alarm is to make sure yours goes off first. I'm kidding, actually. Alarmingly, this isn't much of an issue. And alarmingly, there are still people reading this blog, despite my bad attempts at jokes.

7. On another similar note, in shared rooms you'll get used to packing your backpack in the dark in the morning. Most travelers sleep in.

8. When booking last minute, usually the cheapest beds are sold out. Be prepared to not pay their lowest advertised price. In the winter, I didn't have a single problem walking in late at night and booking for that night, but availability may be more limited in the summer – my friend Jonas loves to tell the story of his first night in NZ, here in Auckland. It was the night of a World Cricket Cup match, which for some inexplicable reason is wildly popular, and all the rooms and beds were sold out except for one for $500. So he had to find a dirt cave under an overpass to spend the night…

9. Some hostels let you set up a tent in their backyard for a significantly cheaper price, while still having access to the facilities. Just ask!

10. Save your meals that require long simmer times for hostels (rice and pasta) to conserve camping fuel.

REAL pasta with FRESH VEGETABLES and a JAR of tomato sauce! A luxury reserved for a hostel kitchen.

11. For some reason, beds on the north island are usually cheaper. You can often find $20 beds in the north, while in the south beds are usually $30.

12. Take advantage of the free food boxes, and get creative with your breakfasts and dinners. Some options: toast with marmalade and peanut butter with a sprinkle of raw sugar, rice pudding made with custard powder and free milk, and (pictured below) cous cous with canned peas.

Yummm! Cous cous with canned "mint flavored" peas, a noodle seasoning packet, and some dried basil. Fo' frizzle!

13. Laundry facilities are usually $4 to wash and $4 to dry, but most have a big sink in the laundry room. Learn to do laundry in the sink and find the clothesline or the drying room. Or get creative finding warm objects – draping clothing over any available heaters is not off limits. I saw a bra on the hallway heater once.

last day in the country!

june 11, 2015

That's right, folks, I'm all packed up and set to leave Aotearoa (the land of the long white cloud, aka New Zealand). See? My Māori is getting better.

Google.co.nz offered in: Māori

Google is so helpful and flattering! It thinks I might want to do my internet searching in Māori 😆

First, though, you can check out some pics of Tongariro on this page and the next since I slighted you earlier.

Because I'd been able to find a ride back to Auckland from the Hot Water Beach, and then cut the Tongariro hike short and caught the bus back to town, I had one more day to head up north of Auckland, up to Paihia.

It wasn't the tourist capital the way many of the other cities in the north island attempted to be (Rotorua, Taupo, etc) but it had a quiet, reserved beauty, and I was surprised by how much history was there! The Bay of Islands, where Paihia is situated, was home to New Zealand's first capital city, and is where the Treaty of Waitangi was signed to give NZ its sovereignty.

Long walk down the access road to the start...

Mt. Ruapeho, home of the ski resort called Whakapapa. This causes endless pausing and giggling, as the "wh" in Māori is pronounced like "f." So the name sounds like...something a "mama" might do.

I didn't properly take heed of this sign, because (a) I had gear and experience and (b) I expected it to clear up. Oh well.

That's where I'm headed! Looks beautiful right now! Tongariro on the left, Mt. Ngauruhoe on the right.

Above, here is the view of Tongariro National Park – a couple of pimples on the flat landscape of the north island. Below, shortly after, the clouds rolling in. I can see why they call it Mt. Doom in LOTR.

I think the highlight of the trip north of Auckland was the scenery on the drive. For four hours, we saw nothing but green rolling hills with some trees and some farm-houses. The hills by themselves aren't spectacular, what is spectacular is that THE WHOLE NORTH ISLAND IS PICTURESQUE. Four hours of unblemished idyllic countryside. Would've liked to continue north to check out 90 Mile Beach too.

I did some day hikes around Paihia, saw the falls, saw the treaty grounds, took a cheap ferry over to Russell, and totally splurged on dinner and bought an awesome

Pano of the Bay of Islands. This place can't be captured by a single photograph - it's so spread out.

A little beach at Tapeka del Mar.

falafel/lamb gyros/chicken wrap while I caught up on some internet. Then, and I know it was 7:35p because my phone had just told me to check in for my flight, I was headed up to my campsite when I ran into a guy asking if I was lost (cause I was looking at my phone). I said no, but then we started chatting.

With really no urging from me, he proceeded to tell me his life story as of 2007, and talked for 3 HOURS. I don't understand people who can just talk…and talk…and talk. I just stand there and listen, and I'm not in a hurry, so I just kind of wait and see how long they can keep it up. No pauses for 3 hours…I think that's a record. His name was Luke, he lives on a yacht on the South Island, and he's been hitchhiking up to a place called Ngawha Spring for some body cleansing. He just spent two un-

Getting close to sunset on the Waitangi River.

planned days at a hippie organic farm in the middle of nowhere, and before this period in his life he had sailed to Vanuatu because before that period he had lived with a Swiss couple who sailed the world and he took care of their kids as they prepared a new boat and told him all about their trips to Vanuatu. And he told me all about his trips into Kahurangi National Park, and the guy he went with one time who almost died from hypothermia.

And I realized I'm just a poser. I'm not a REAL vagabond, and I don't think I'll ever be. I occasionally find free places to sleep, but very well hidden and out of town. This guy finds free MEALS, and his favorite places to sleep are in churches, in bowling greens (because the old people who use them never wake up early he says), or get this, under the awnings at kindergartens.

As an aside, on the ferry to Russell, I was inspired to compose for y'all a list of the **Top 5 Nerdy Moments** for my trip here:

1. On the ferry, we passed a ferry going the other direction. I got so excited to watch our wakes make a cool Moiré pattern in the water. Also reminded me of watching a really cool three dimensional sinusoidal animation in Mathematica.

The peaceful town of Russell 🙂

So peaceful! Clearly the ducks aren't worried about being washed over the waterfall. Maybe they're adrenaline junkies!

I've never seen a mangrove forest before! All the tree roots have heaps of tiny fingers that stick up through the mud, and are set up to take advantage of being submerged twice a day from the tidal variation.

Haruru Falls

2. I was drying my hands under a really high-speed air hand dryer in Rotorua and had way too much fun playing with the Bernoulli effect, feeling my hands get sucked together by the high velocity air.

3. Matching the resonant frequency of one of the new suspension bridges on the Heaphy Track by bouncing up and down, and getting enough amplitude that I legitimately worried myself.

4. Hearing a bird here in the north island in Russell and realizing its call sounds exactly like a dub step break.

5. Being disappointed that the pdf I put on my eReader titled "An Introduction to General Relativity" didn't format properly and is consequently unreadable.

top 9 things i didn't get to see/do

june 11, 2015

First things first. Random thing I'm proud of today: I set a new personal best time on my Sudoku app! I won't tell you how long it is, though, because I'm still so slow it's embarrassing.

So now that I'm back in the states, I can reminisce about my trip. And start complaining that it's too hot and dry here ☼

But seriously, if you've read through some of the stuff I've written, my hope is that you can use that a bit as a guide to help decide some places you'd like to go or see when you head over to NZ. However, there are some places that I didn't make it to but would have liked to. I'll list em out, and you can tell me about them if you get a chance to check them out (or if you have already).

1. **Catlins** – This is a place, way down by Invercargill, that I didn't hear about until a couple weeks into my trip. I didn't read about it in any of my planning, but I repeatedly heard from people how cool it was.

2. **Milford Track** – All of the point-to-point hiking tracks (as opposed to loops) are logistically difficult to arrange transportation for, since you end up a different place than where you start, often a few hours by car. Milford Track ups the ante, though, because you need to get a boat to the start, and a boat from the end at a different body of water. Additionally, the winter rain often floods and closes the track. Somehow, the huts get fully booked up to six months in advance.

3. **Stewart Island** – Heard nothing but good things about Stewart Island. The whole island is a national park! However, winter is not the best time. Since it's so far south it gets quite cold, and it's so untamed I heard from a friend here that he spent 9-10 days on a tramp there, with mud up to his thighs. It is a cool place to catch a glimpse of the southern lights though.

4. **Arthur's Pass** – Would have been pretty cool, and you can see the snow-capped mountains from either coast, but my bus line didn't have service there, and it was quite a detour from traveling up the west coast. Decided to do Heaphy Track instead, and experience tropical rainforest instead of more mountains.

5. **Southern Lights** – STILL HAVENT SEEN ANY LIGHTS IN THE SKY. So bummed. You need three conditions: extreme enough latitude, dark enough sky (winter), and no clouds. New Zealand is about the closest to the equator where you can see them, and occasionally you can see them as far north as Queenstown. In Alaska, you have to be there in winter for it to be dark enough (and who really wants that?)

6. **Tongariro Alpine Crossing** – Yeah, sure, I got almost halfway, and many would say I did the best half, but I couldn't see a darn thing. And it was only almost halfway. There was still quite a bit of walking around in the craters at the top.

7. **Rob Roy glacier in Mt. Aspiring National Park** – it's an hour from town by car, over gravel roads and fording a few rivers, and given that it had rained every day I was nearby I was told the road was probably impassable.

8. **Cape Reinga** – where the two oceans meet, the Tasman Sea and the Pacific Ocean. I'm told it's quite beautiful, with a lighthouse, but there's no bus service and I didn't have time to hitchhike it.

9. **Equippers Church in Auckland** – I had a chance to spend time at the Equippers churches in both Dunedin and Wellington, and both were amazing, friendly, and small, congregations with GREAT music. The Auckland church is much much bigger, and I would have loved to check it out.

But ya know what? As long as I stayed busy every day and I was doing what I wanted, I'm totally happy. Maybe I didn't see everything I wanted to, but even the people who are here for MONTHS don't see everything they want to. I haven't even seen everything I want to in California, and I've lived there for my whole life! As long as I'm out here instead of behind a desk, right now that's enough for me ☺

chapter 2: the long walk
hiking the pacific crest trail

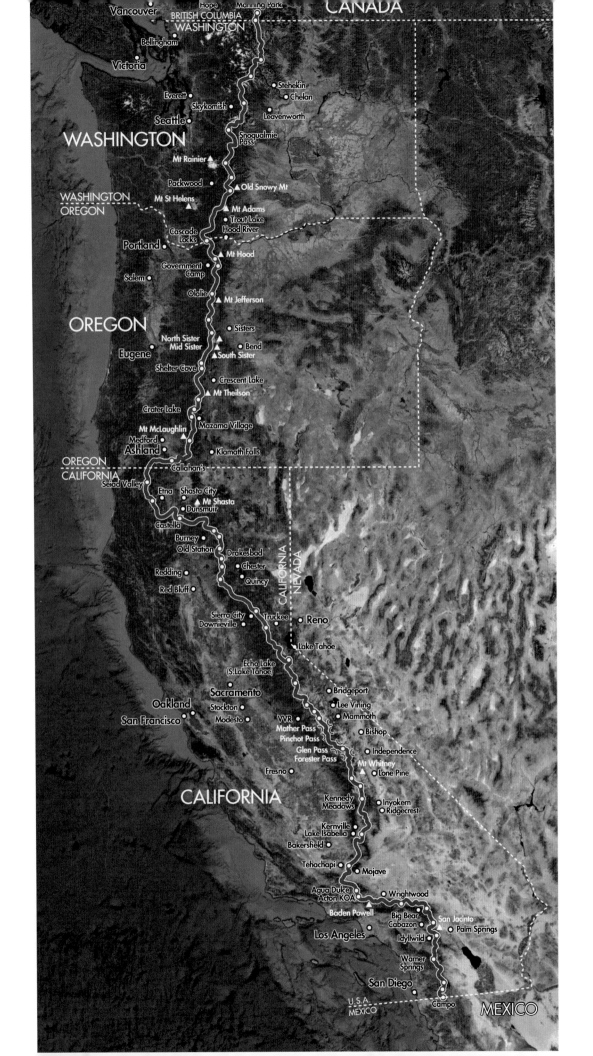

on the trail, SOBO 2015!

july 5, 2015

Well, I didn't make a post before I left because (no surprise!) I was busy with last minute prep, filling Mom's house with food and camping gear as I packed. Now, bear with me here: I've uploaded additional nature pics to my Flickr account so you don't have to sift through mountains of commentary to see the pics, or vice versa (like how I squeezed two puns into one sentence there?). I'll keep the blog mainly for pictures with a story - there's just far too much beautiful scenery. Full Flickr album here: https://flic.kr/s/aHskfBrVb6

On June 22, I got some family to drive me from Bellingham to the trailhead at Harts Pass, Washington, where I would walk north to the Canadian border, flip a U-turn, and start a long walk south to the Mexican border along the Pacific Crest Trail. And I've meant to make some posts along the way, but that's proving trickier than expected. I haven't spent more than half a day at any of the small towns I've passed through, all with limited cell coverage, and most of my time spent doing in-town chores and hanging out with fellow crazy hiker friends.

My itinerary took me north from Harts Pass to the border after spending the night camped at the pass with my Washington family. Snow reports had said that the snow level would be pretty low, and the pass road had opened up a few weeks earlier than normal, but most of the hikers had brought micro spikes and an ice axe to the trailhead. After talking to locals and looking at the (apparently) summer conditions, pretty much everyone left their winter gear behind. In the first few hours of hiking, I passed a handful of hikers on their way back from the border already – seems that a biggish group had started three days before me, on Friday, and I'd be chasing them for a while. Just a couple hours in, I ran into a guy who wasn't doing so well, and he was on his way south. He had brought awful food (mostly protein bars with some freeze dried dinners), an extra 30 lbs of photography equipment, and was planning 10-14 day food drops. He hadn't done much training before the trip, and had just quit smoking when he flew out of Ohio. He was having trouble keeping food down, so he hadn't eaten in a day and a half. Helped him get his pack to the base of the pass, got him some REAL food (pepperoni and gummy candies, yum), and tried to get him to promise me he would take the rest of the day off. It was heartbraking because you could tell he was absolutely LOVING the scenery and the experience, but he couldn't handle the

This will be my life for a while.

Still smiling! Oh wait, I haven't started yet...

This is my best "oh well! Here goes nothing!" pose.

94

weight and the exertion. He thought he was gonna quit, but I told him to spend a day thinking about it, and mail the camera stuff home, and get some real food. My legs were fresh, so I covered the distance from the pass to the border and back in two days and camped at Windy Pass, a few miles north of Harts, with a batch of new recruits headed to the border the next day.

Stehekin was the first resupply, and boy was I looking forward to it! I had opted for Gore-Tex shoes for the first stretch of the hike, in anticipation of snow and cold, but the lack of snow and the unseasonably early heat wave pushing the temps to the low 90s had my feet absolutely sweltering and soaked with sweat, causing me to stop every couple hours to cool them off and dry everything out. At Stehekin I had a pair of mesh trail-runners waiting for me. Also, everyone I talked to couldn't help but GUSH about the amazing bakery there. About two days before Stehekin, I caught up with a hiker who'd started before me, and we leap-frogged with each other the last miles into town. His "name" was Pan, cause he played a pan flute every morning and night wherever he camped, and I got to hear his crazy life adventure story over a few hours of our hiking.

Stehekin was awesome! It's a little community that's accessible only by hiking along the PCT, or a long ferry ride down Lake Chelan, so it feels like a summer camp for adults. Everyone working there is smiling, not from a keep-the-tourists-happy kind of smile, but because they really want to be there. Pan and I did laundry and swam, and later in the afternoon a few other hiker friends rolled in on the afternoon shuttle from the trail. We all went through our boxes together, and at the post office there was a sign advertising "Juggling Night! On Friday, 6pm." As luck would have it, that night was Friday, and Peter was a very skilled juggler, so the whole town of Stehekin got together on the lawn and juggled, and slack-lined, and Peter impressed us by juggling SEVEN BALLS!

Turned out all the campgrounds were full, so they let us sleep on the front lawn of the ranger/visitor station (which turned out to be much better than the campground anyway, in all of our opinions).

Next day we rented bikes to ride out to the falls, grabbed some cinnamon rolls and sticky buns for resupply, and met this crazy boar-hunting, conspiracy theorist, pot-smoking, swearing chiropractor who hung out with us and "readjusted" our bodies while complaining about how much we were screwing ourselves up 😄

Making a fashion statement with my grandma's disposable roll-up sunglasses and my sun-brella 😎

These flowers remind me of "The Lorax" by Dr. Seuss. Anyone else see that?

Hanging out on the front lawn of the ranger station, unpacking boxes, while Pan turns his sleep pad into a multipurpose hitchhiking sign.

More than one hiker has fallen in love with the community and stayed a few extra days, giving it the nickname "Stuck-hekin," but Peter and I broke away that afternoon to get in about 10 miles for the day. Pan had to stay behind because the foam on the left half of one of the heels of his shoe had collapsed, giving him some knee problems, so his sister was overnighting him another while he wrote a "strongly worded letter" to the shoe company. I was still having shoe problems of my own – even though my new mesh shoes were an improvement, my inflamed and blistered feet had swollen up an extra shoe size, so they were feeling pretty cramped.

Peter is a physics major (and quite a nerd) so we played some word games while we hiked that evening. Next morning we split up to hike at our own paces, and a few days later I hit Stevens Pass. That day, who should I run into but the hiker from the first day who I had been able to help out! He was so excited to see me, and was so proud to tell me he had bought a bunch of pepperoni and gummy candies that he carried with him now ☺ He had mailed most of his stuff home and gotten a ride a bit up the trail, to Rainy Pass, which is how he'd gotten in front of me. A short hitchhike brought me into Skykomish, where there was purported to be a magical place called the "Dinsmore's Hiker Haven." Andrea and Jerry Dinsmore had a small piece of land, a big metal garage converted into a dorm-style room with bunk beds, a kitchenette, fridge, couches, and a TV, with free shower and laundry facilities. And in the evening, they

Peter had the great idea to ship himself Nutella in emptied toothpaste tubes! He says it kinda leaves the Nutella with a minty flavor, I say he can brush his teeth with Nutella and avoid bringing toothpaste!

The famous cinnamon rolls. I did try to eat it without getting any icing in my beard, but of course I failed. I hope I don't have any bears come and try and lick my face tonight.

Rainbow Falls in Stehekin with Adam and Peter.

Peter juggling SEVEN!!

grilled burgers! I was really surprised when I saw some fellow hikers roll in who I had passed a while back… they were doing half the miles a day I was, and should have been a couple days behind me still. But I guess they were creative with their route-finding skills and took a few sections of the "old PCT" that forded rivers instead of going miles out of the way to the nearest bridge and made up the time on me. One of them, Jolly Rancher, was an Afghanistan army vet who was doing the hike with his service dog, a great big white Pyrenees mountain dog named Shadow. This guy had all SORTS of stories, and the two guys he was hiking with, Wade and Gator, seemed like they had known each other for years, even though they had just met a few days back in Stehekin. Wade and Gator had done the Appalachian Trail last summer, and the Florida Trail this past winter, and apparently that wasn't enough so here they were on the PCT this year.

From Stehekin I had ordered a size bigger shoes from REI to be delivered here in Skykomish, so I was excited to get those out on the trail. I said goodbye to everyone and started walking again. I was told this stretch would be a busy one, because Snoqualmie Pass, on I-90, is the easiest access to the PCT from Seattle so you have lots of sectioners, day hikers, trail runners, etc. I had a few issues on the trail this stretch, though. This was the first stretch I hadn't brought a set of paper maps, and coincidentally this was the first stretch that had an "alternate route" option. Soooo…I didn't really know much about the alternate, but there were a few signs on the main trail (and on my phone!) warning about a "dangerous river ford" two miles ahead. I had heard there would be river fordings on the trail, but so far all the crossings had had a log over them, or stones, or something, so I didn't know what to make of this. I also thought of my friends who had saved like 20 miles of trail by taking the adventurous route. So, I figured I'd have to get my feet wet at some point and set on ahead to the "dangerous ford." Which proved to be not bad, but would have been very dangerous indeed earlier in the season. Armed with this new confidence, at the next "alternate," I was like "psh! Please, I'm a PCT purist now, no alternates for me." Only that alternate it turns out saves about 10 miles and like 6000ft of hot dry switchbacks. So I'm kind of bummed I didn't take that one, but because I stuck to the trail I got to meet and camp with Kevin and Lisa (from Modesto, IL! Sister city!) who showed me some wild blueberries to pick (or maybe they were huckleberries? The PNW has so many unusual varieties of berries!) and I spent my last day before Snoqualmie leap-frogging with a fellow thru-hiker named Jill and having some good conver-

What's this a picture of, you say? Why, it's the trail! It's somewhere in there, I promise. It was through a stretch like this I lost a sock that was drying, off the back of my pack.

Hm…outHOUSE? Might be a little generous. Maybe more like outBOX. But either way, it beats digging a hole.

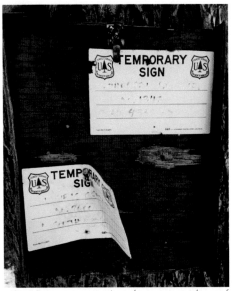

"Temporary Sign" must mean it's only temporarily useful…just until the Sharpie fades.

sations. I got a lot of compliments on my sun umbrella that I used during the 20 miles of exposed hot dry ridge traverses ☼

Snoqualmie was my first resupply I hadn't intended to spend the night at, but my right Achilles has swollen up, so I'm chillin here today, checking out the pancake house, brewery, and writing out this blog post while I post up at the trailhead.

Gear's working out good, other than the shoes, and I've actually avoided two thunderstorms that people camping nearby (like on the other side of a ridge) said brought rivers through their tents, but I only got a couple hours of drizzling. So I think I'm going to swap my water resistant bivy for a mosquito bivy, as that seems like it'd be FAR more useful. My 20° bag is much too hot at night, but my shoulders are getting eaten alive by the bugs 🕷

Learning to eat with a bug head-net on. A useful skill!

My sister wanted to see an example of what I'm eating out here. On the left, trail food. On the right, town food.

From top to bottom: Diablo Lake on Hwy 20 near Rainy Pass, looking north over Hopkins Lake towards Canada, and two views looking north from Hart's Pass. The North Cascades in springtime are absolutely stunning.

Clockwise, from top: more stunning views of the North Cascades, prepared for rain under my tarp at Hopkins Lake, a forested valley in the Cascades, and Monument 78 - the northern terminus of the trail on the US/Canada border.

Clockwise, from top: an enormous glacial valley near Glacier Peak, Mica Lake, wildflowers in the North Cascades, and my campsite just north of Cutthroat Pass at sunset.

the kracker barrel

Got in to White Pass today, and am only now realizing that apparently all of the towns in Washington that the trail passes through are actually ski resorts, which makes sense as they are the highest points in the mountains with any services. I have really been impressed by the services provided by all these stops, after being warned that there will be pretty much nothing at any of them. I look forward now to a nice meal at each and maybe a cool place to stay with friends.

Ha, White Pass is different. There is NOTHING here. The gas station/post office/restaurant is proud (or rather, reluctant) to serve microwave burritos and maybe a microwaved burger from their freezer section. But they did begrudgingly make a nice large pizza for me and a friend to split, and the allure of splitting a small motel room was irresistible after the brief afternoon thunderstorm and the realization that my clothes haven't been washed in weeks and won't be for another week.

Wait, don't get me wrong. I had a BLAST in the afternoon thunderstorm. Ya know why?? That's right, cause I had my umbrella. And it's earned me the trail name Shade cause it got me so many comments on the long hot sunny traverse about a week ago.

I spent the last four days since Snoqualmie hiking with a new trail friend Cookie! We met up on the way through the Alpine Lakes Wilderness just north of Snoqualmie, and my zero day there set us back on schedule. She had friends visiting her from Seattle, so we all ate at the brewery before putting in about 4 miles on the trail to get us out of town. Our paces worked well together for that stretch, so we had lots of fun over the next four days playing some word games/20 questions while chasing the "Cascadia" footprints (a recognizable brand of shoe) on the trail that always just seem to be a day ahead of us, and following the trail of pistachio shells that some hiker has been leaving, hoping to ascertain the identity of each. We started encountering our first northbound thru hikers a few days ago, and boy do they look ragged. Good talking to them though.

I'm in a hurry to get to Cascade Locks by the 15th to meet up with mom and aunt driving up, but there's been a snag – our first trail closure due to fire is waiting for us on the next stretch, just west of, and at the base of, Mt. Adams. Bit of a bummer, as the detour removes 4 of the most beautiful miles of the stretch and replaces it with 15 miles of side trails and gravel roads. But what can ya do.

Internet here is pretty low quality, but I'll try to put up some pics later.

Looking west towards Mt. Rainer as the sun sets.

so long, washington!
july 16, 2015

Resurfaced yesterday in Cascade Locks, OR, crossing the majestically named Bridge of the Gods over the Columbia River Gorge to leave Washington behind. Legend has it that a long time ago a landslide here obscured the river. The river then bored a hole through the landslide, leaving behind a natural bridge for the native Americans to cross on, hence "Bridge of the Gods." Though this one is very much man-made and composed entirely of steel. People had told me crossing the bridge was the most dangerous stretch of the trail, but I thought they were joking. Turns out it's only barely wide enough for two cars, and there's no sidewalk. Add traffic both ways, metal grate flooring, and gusty wind, and I can kind of see what they're talking about. Apparently the toll for pedestrians is $0.50, but they didn't seem to care that I just walked right past the tollbooth. I'm such a lawbreaker.

Anyway! I have some unfinished business left over from White Pass, where I promised pictures. Check out the latest batch here: https://flic.kr/s/aHskfGqC4X

And now, the awards. Improvised gear of the week award goes to the "Maxipack" for the creative use of feminine hygiene products (Maxipads) as self-adhesive supplemental padding for shoulders and hip belts on the backpack. They absorb sweat and stick surprisingly well!

Award for "Appropriate Song of the Day" goes to The Proclaimers for their hit single "I Would Walk 500 Miles" (you know the song).

Award for best mom ever goes to MY MOM who does an awesome job packing and sending me resupply boxes. She tells me that she and my grandma have fun little packing parties where they take my spreadsheet "food order" and measure everything out and then throw in a cute note or something. I think Amazon can learn a thing or two from her.

Highlights from the last week on the trail include spectacular views of Mt. Adams, even though we had to detour off the mountain for the fire closure, meeting a Scottish couple on the forest road who gave me a hitch past the closure (they were on a round-the-world trip, currently driving from Seattle to Portland, and GPS had routed them through the MIDDLE OF NOWHERE for 40 miles on this dirt road, but boy was I grateful), the Knife's Edge in the Goat Rocks Wilderness where I met

Backpacking is all about multipurpose gear. These pads are good for, apart from the obvious use, extra padding, an absorbent dressing for wounds, and can you think of anything else?

This sign attests to the fact that I know what it's like to walk 500 miles. And I will walk 500 more.

Would you believe I've never had huckleberries before??

a 74 y/o lady with her kids backpacking over this epic terrain, and definitely the tremendous amount of wild berries to pick along the trail. I had no idea the staggering variety of berries here in the PNW (that's Pacific Northwest, folks). From the unusual (black caps, thimble berries, marionberries, huckleberries, salmonberries) to the typical (blueberries, raspberries, blackberries, strawberries), if you keep your eyes peeled, you can keep your mouth satisfied. Thanks, Cookie, for teaching me to look around me at the plants and animals! Still working on focusing a little ways down the trail without tripping on what's right in front of me though.

Speaking of not being great at walking yet, we did the math. You know how they say you need to do something for 10,000 hours to be an expert? Turns out I won't even be an expert hiker after all this. At thirteen hours a day for a hundred and twenty days, that's only 1560 hours. Even a triple crowner (someone who hikes the Pacific Crest Trail, the Appalachian Trail, and the Continental Divide Trail) probably isn't an "expert." So I don't feel too bad calling myself a rookie ☺

I'm convinced no one actually likes walking 30 miles a day. Or thirteen hours. But people like the experience of the trail, they like covering the distance to the next place, they like watching the landscape change. It's great to be covering so much distance you can watch the environment change around you. Or look back at a viewpoint to a particularly iconic peak that looks SO FAR AWAY and say…"dude, I was there 2 days ago."

The experience of walking somewhere instead of driving makes the camaraderie among hikers that much better, and it makes the food taste that much better in town. There are trail angels who open their homes and facilities to the hikers, and people are so nice and helpful.

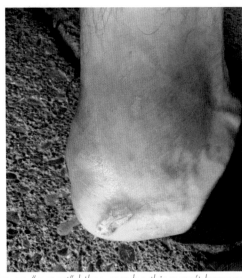

When I'm an "expert" hiker, maybe this won't happen, but until then my Achilles hates me, and Vitamin "I" (ibuprofen) is my friend.

There's a guy here named Joe Shelley, known as "Shrek," who after having to drop out of his hike due to an injury, moved to Cascade Locks just to be a trail angel. He calls his house "Shrek's Swamp," and is working on building a replica of Shrek's underground swamp house in the hillside behind his house. Hikers have access to laundry and shower facilities, electricity for charging devices, and a free place to camp.

Zoom way in here. See the snow capped lone peak, righting the center, amidst the clouds? That's Mt. Adams. I was there 2 days ago, by walking! It's unreal!

If I'm getting tired of walking towards the end of the day, it's a great pick-me-up to pass a northbounder and talk to them for a few minutes. Everyone wants to know who and what is ahead of them on the trail, and it's fun to keep track of the few people ahead of and behind you. For the past three weeks I've been trailing two guys named Green Mile and Sailor, by just a few miles. Every person coming north would tell me they're just a few hours ahead of me, but I didn't meet them until yesterday, crossing the bridge into Cascade Locks, and I felt kind of like I knew them. Even though I feel like I know the few people on either side of me, every town I make a few new friends. Really interested to see what it's like passing "the herd" of northbounders halfway through Oregon. Supposedly they issued 2000 northbound permits this year, so it's gonna be crazy.

I give this section of trail going into Mt. Rainier National Park a big thumbs up.

Family is great 😊

We'll make a "guest award" category and call it the "Lucky Shot of the Day award." The morning fog and trees and sun aligned for about 30 seconds, and I pulled out my phone just in time.

I put this picture on my Flickr feed, but it probably doesn't make any sense unless I explain it: I thought it was hilarious that the post said "Locate Sign"...and all I could think was "I did it! I located the sign! It's right here!" Okay, I give up. Another waste of pixels.

So THIS is where the other shooter was... (ya know, JFK? Okay bad joke, waste of camera pixels)

skiers, and bike racers, and lava fields

july 24, 2015

Album for this section: https://flic.kr/s/aHskge91Ef

After spending a couple days off in Cascade Locks (during which I got to take my first trip out on a small sailboat!), I was still inexplicably feeling the need to stick to my "schedule." It was meant to be descriptive, not prescriptive, but it's weird how humans have a need for (or at least I have a need for) order, or a plan, or semblance of control. Anyway, this perceived need to stick to my schedule, combined with the fact that my legs were now fresh, combined with the reports from the northbounders I was encountering that "Oregon was all flat, and great for 35 mile days," got me all worked up to make it to my next stop, Timberline Lodge, in a half day less than planned. This also worked well, because I would make it there by nightfall, camp, then hit up the legendary allyoucaneat breakfast buffet. Seriously, every northbounder I encountered told me about this breakfast buffet – $15 for all you can eat made from scratch amazing gourmet breakfast foods. And these hikers can eat A LOT.

The Oregon stretch of the trail has a lot more "alternate" sections than Washington, that go briefly away from the main trail for water or past a scenic area, and I took two of them on this stretch. Everyone recommended Eagle Creek instead of the main trail leaving Cascade Locks, and it was delightful, and I also chose to walk past Ramona Falls. Both alternates are highly recommended by me, but then I didn't take the PCT for these small sections, so my recommendation doesn't really mean much lol.

The alternates have a different "feel" than the PCT: they are built to different standards – wider, smoother, no tree blazes, gentler grade – and the people traveling them are very different from PCT hikers, usually day hikers or weekend backpackers. It felt like coming home to an old friend to get back on the PCT ☺

Anyway, rolled into Timberline in time to pick up my resupply package, rummage through the SPECTAC-ULAR hiker box, and hang out in the lodge area for a couple hours before walking just up the hill a short ways to camp. The breakfast buffet was all it was talked up to be (which was amazing in itself), and I had delightful hiker company with a hiker named Hakuna Matata as I ate my six plates of food.

Here's Punchbowl Falls, on the Eagle Creek trail. The PCT rarely, if ever, "follows" creeks, instead preferring the ridgeline. This was a nice change.

Ramona Falls was the most unique falls on the trail, well worth the trip!

First view of Mt. Hood!

The sign at Timberline (Mt. Hood) tells me I'm making progress!

One of the lava fields I had to walk through. The lava rocks tear up your shoes!

Another awesome sight along Eagle Creek was Tunnel Falls, where the trail actually goes through a tunnel behind the falls.

So one of the draws of Timberline Lodge, that sits on Mt. Hood, is that there is "skiing year round." It was definitely weird seeing everyone in their ski gear, tromping around the dirty and dry parking lot, heading up the hill onto a thumbnail sized patch of dirty snow. But there were LOTS of skiers. I was surprised.

The next surprise was getting a phone call from my friend Chuck, who was in Portland (!) and asked me where I was. I told him I was at Mt. Hood, and it turns out he was picking up his girlfriend from the airport and they were headed south to Bend so she could compete in a high profile national cycling race. I said I would hurry down there and meet them in (checks schedule…) 4 days! Cause I can do bigger mileage in Oregon and chop a whole day off my schedule, right?

So. I've now committed myself to 33 mi/day pace for the next 4 days. But Oregon is flat and easy, right? LOL! Turns out those next 4 days were the most difficult, mountainous, and rocky stretch of Oregon. So I pretty much wore myself out, and had to start doubling my food rations.

But I dragged myself into McKenzie Pass at Hwy 242 which would take me to Sisters, then onto Bend. I was having trouble hitching a ride, so I started walking up the road a bit, only to discover I was at the summit finish of the first stage of the bike race, and the women's field was going to be coming through in about 30 mins! So the race promoters gave me a soda and some chips and I met up with Chuck and Leah up there on the pass 🚴

The race is a 5 day affair, and I was hoping to stay for the whole thing, but at this point things started to get real uncomfortable and awkward. Leah's team was staying in a host family's house, so I wasn't really welcome, and I didn't have transportation to get to and from the races since the team vehicles were full. Also, Chuck had not actually taken the time off of work so he was glued to his computer screen every spare moment. And I have to say, this is the first time I've felt unwelcome and homeless in a town/city in over two months of being homeless. Bend has no camping, no hostels, very few motels and most full, and it is not a hiker friendly or traveler friendly location.

So I awkwardly stretched out my welcomes as long as possible, staying on a couch and squeezing into a race vehicle, but it was clear after the first day I was in the way and needed to get out of there. Chuck drove me back to Sisters, we had a burger, and he said bye. I immediately

And my first trail magic, just south of Mt. Washington! Too bad all the snacks had been eaten ☹ I was actually much more excited to find an unopened gallon of water at the trailhead a mile later, cause it had been a long dry stretch.

What an insane coincidence! This is exactly where I popped out from the trail, and just at the right time!

Here is a picture of what I was in the way of ☹

felt better in Sisters once I found out they had a city run campground with a $5 hiker/biker spot. But then I felt bummed again when I realized I'd left my sun hat in Bend ☹

So I'm all set to spend the night here, then grab my re-supply tomorrow when the post office opens, buy another hat, and hitch back to the trail. Overall I would say it was a useful experience, but it was my first negative experience here on my trip.

Oh! And some highlights from the last week. Definitely running into a dad and his 7 year old son out for a 50 mile backpack trip! In five days! Kid was loving it, and told me all about how he wanted to make a Minecraft mod (a popular video game) about the trip when he got home 😀

And, when a Todd poops in the woods, is there anyone there to see it? Well, almost never. I got caught, and about a mile from a youth camp, lol. I usually prop my backpack on the side of the trail and walk a ways off, but some hikers going by, instead of figuring out what this meant, strained their eyes to look deep into the woods to see where the pack's owner was. And then, once spotting me, still not picking up on the cues, proceeded to say hi to me. Ummm....oh well 😆

Top: Mt. Adams, Bottom: Knife's Edge in Goat Rocks Wilderness

crater lake! and trail angels! and coming home!

august 3, 2015

First, a couple songs that have been on my mind:

As I was hiking into the Ashland area, the sky just filled up with smoke over the course of about a day and a half, and it got really thick, almost foggy. I had this line of lyrics running through my head that went like "with the smoke filling my lungs." Took me a lot of humming and thinking and hiking to remember that that line was from a song called "The Good Life" by a band called Boxer & Clover. As I listen to it now, I realize the line is actually "with the FUMES filling my lungs." I'm listening again to the song now, and I haven't heard it in a long time. It's a cool song about how hometowns, though they can be tiresome and not where you wanna be in life, are still home. Oddly relevant, check it out: http://youtu. be/_Q35tocOt78

Next song is called "Welcome Home" by Radical Face. As I prepare to walk into California sometime in the next two days, I feel like I'm returning home, in a way ☺ A very dreamy song, I think you'll like it: http://youtu. be/P8a4iiOnzsc

Now, the picture album from this last week and a half in Oregon: https://flic.kr/s/aHskdVnUrz

When I left you guys last, I was a bit bummed from my time in Bend, but looking forward to a night in Sisters. I'm really starting to appreciate my time in these small trail communities, many of which you can hardly even call towns. Sisters had a city run campground right in town with a hiker biker spot, and the post office was walking distance away the next morning. I didn't even have to wait long for a ride to the trail, because a sweet older lady named Blanche drives back and forth between town and the trailhead, looking for hikers to give rides to, and she took me on up 🚗

Oregon has been a bit different from Washington in terms of resupply locations – while in Washington they were mostly ski resorts, in Oregon they're mostly lake resorts, and there is something like every 50 miles it seems like, so lots of people do like 3 day food carries and go into most of the lake resorts. I passed most of them by, but one place I was curious about was Shelter Cove, which also happened to be along an alternate I was

Spent the night in Sisters with these bikers. Three of them were four days away from finishing their transamerica bike ride, the fourth was from Bend, and was just riding with them for a day. They told me if you give the Sheriffs dept a heads up, you can often camp in city parks.

The mountains in Oregon known as "The Three Sisters" were great. Looks like one of "the sisters" has her head in the clouds.

interested in checking out. Coming into the resort on the trail there was a cute little handwritten note advertising a trail angel named Peggy with a phone number. I was looking forward to ice cream at the store when I got in, but they closed early so I was a bit bummed. But I did meet some northbounders who had given this trail angel a call, saying there were about 4 or 5 of us who were looking for a place to stay for the night. She drove on up in a station wagon, and told us to pile in! She had a cabin up the road and she'd take us to the "better" store a ways up the road.

What a wild ride! We had more people than seatbelts, and we were bottoming the suspension on the lumpy road. The speedometer on her car was broken, but I don't think she knew what a speedometer was for…gas pedal was on the floor the whole time and we were FLYING! We got to the store, got some communal ice cream and beer, and she bought a Marie Calendars apple pie to bake. The cabin was….homey….and smelled like cats (to put it nicely) but she was so happy to host us, and we all took showers and she did our laundry. She told us we were free to smoke whatever we wanted in the house, which a few of the guys promptly took her up on (surprisingly common out here…) And then we all had pie and ice cream 🍰 I've decided hanging out with north-bounders is a pain, because whenever we "draw straws" to have to do something, it always goes to "the person who's walked the least amount of miles," i.e. me. She woke up bright and early and RACED us out to the trailhead, before heading back home to go back to sleep lol.

Those two experiences with trail angels kind of changed my perspective on trail angels. I'd kind of thought of them as "people who are willing to help if you need it." But more and more, I see that they're "people who want to meet hikers," oftentimes mother hen type figures who

Springs are something that literally blow my mind. They just start…out of nowhere and make awesome water.

Random "high"-light is the highest point on the trail for all of Washington and Oregon. Didn't expect it to be in Oregon! As a bonus you can see me all decked out in my sun protection (hat, sunglasses, long sleeves, pants, and sun gloves). They don't call me Shade for nuthin'. Also, you can see why a mom referred to me as a "trail man" to her kid.

IT'S SO PRETTY. And you can see Mt. Shasta off there to the right, way off in the distance. At least until the smoke rolled in a day later.

Celebrating my bday in Crater Lake! My mom sent me a special care package 🖤

And she made me take a selfie with the disguise she sent me 😎 *NO ONE WILL RECOGNIZE ME!*

Definitely the most scenic part of the trip so far…walking on a highway, next to I-5, in thick smoke, for the half mile into Callahans.

love to talk and take care of people. They brag about how many people they meet, and how much fun it is. They truly WANT you to give them a call! And they usually love to tell you all about their life story 😊

My favorite places in Oregon so far have been Jefferson Park and the Three Sisters Wilderness. Seriously, check them out if you can.

After Shelter Cove, I made tracks for Crater Lake. This has been like a singular obsession of mine this trip, I've been waiting and anticipating seeing Crater Lake again, ever since visiting it last summer on my road trip.

Having attempted a few times to get a "35" (a 35 mile day) while hurrying to Bend, but only managing 33, I finally was stoked to get a 36 mile day on my way to CL. Apparently because of Oregon's flat terrain, people blow through it pretty fast – there's something referred to as "the two week challenge," to do Oregon in two weeks. And apparently the fastest guys do it in 12 days. Whatever. This is the kind of talk you get when you're towards the front of the pack, and it appears that despite my best efforts to slow down, I'm about 6th or so out of the southbounders. A few of my friends on this last stretch finally got their first "40," but I decided I won't let myself get sucked into that mileage game, or I'll end up killing myself, ha.

But! Got into CL ahead of schedule, and had to hike through my first long dry stretches. While trail talk in Washington and northern Oregon is about food, trail talk in southern Oregon is definitely about water. Longest carry so far is 26 miles without water, and I'm getting pretty good at drinking two liters of water at a time when I get to a spring, then hiking with a sloshing stomach.

I have to say, Crater Lake holds a special place for me still, but I'm not sure why…it just…is magical. When I first got to the rim, I was just hanging out, absorbing it, and started talking to a family. The dad, when they were ready to leave, insisted I take $20 and some water and beef sticks. And then, that night at dinner when I planned to spend it, I made friends with a couple and they bought my dinner without me realizing it. The trail is showing me all the beautifulness of humanity and I love it. Everyone out here is AWESOME.

That brings me to Ashland! Wasn't sure what to expect, but I was hearing from everyone that I HAD to go into town, and there's a cool hiker friendly resort here called

Callahan's with (you guessed it!) an allyoucaneat spaghetti dinner, camping on the lawn, laundry and shower, then allyoucaneat pancakes in the morning. It was overpriced, but they are so friendly and it was a great experience. After that I popped into Ashland, and it happened to be a Sunday so I found a local church. They made a big scene of introducing me during the service, but there was cake afterwards so it was all worth it. And a guy told me to give him a call when I was ready to go back to the trailhead that afternoon ☺

So I spoiled myself in Ashland for my bday and went a saw a movie! In an air conditioned theater! Lol, Mission Impossible was pretty fun to watch ☺ Did I mention there's been a heat wave here? Ugh.

I think I'll do a little awards ceremony for some of the signs I've seen along the trail.

Here's a milestone from the last stretch. See how everything is always about the northbounders? I'm only 1/3 done, thankyouverymuch.

Least Useful (simply says "3")

Most No-Nonsense ("TRAIL")

Best "Hiker Addition" (at this confusing junction somebody added "NOT PCT")

Oddest Lake Name ("Nip and Tuck")

Most Appreciated ("WATER!")

Best Trailside Sculpture

special california edition

august 5, 2015

Wow, I feel like enough has happened in the last three days to merit a special edition. First off: I know Oregon has this whole "nice" culture thing, but even the graffiti is positive!

I had the best birthday present ever when I crossed the California/Oregon border about 7:30p on Aug 3!

I'd also been waiting to hit "the herd" of northbounders, and today was definitely the peak. A few different factors this year caused the herd to spread out considerably, such as early snow in the Sierras causing people to skip ahead, and the fact that the PCTA spread out the permit start dates throughout all of April instead of bunching them up on April 1. Because of this, some people were saying that I wouldn't EVER encounter a herd. But the stream of northbounders grew from a trickle starting in mid Washington to about 20 a day by mid Oregon, to a peak on the 3rd of about 60 northbounders in one day.

The next destination along the town is the "very small community" of Seiad Valley (pop. 350), nestled next to the Shasta Trinity wilderness and right along the Klamath River. Heading south out of Ashland, the Rogue River National Forest was a breath of fresh air from the arid, enclosed, and dusty landscape of southern Oregon. But of course, not literally. As I mentioned earlier, the whole area has filled up with smoke in the past few days, mainly from a large fire in the Grants Pass area but fueled by numerous smaller fires being started all the time from the thunderstorms that have been going on for the past week. So it was a bit of a bummer to be walking along

So Oregon's motto is "You're in Oregon. Be nice." Apparently even the graffiti artists take it to heart.

Best bday present ever! Guess this means I can stop being nice now. Phew! That was getting exhausting.

My first stocked trail magic! In the Rogue River Natl Forest. ▶

And how could I pass this one up?

this ridge in California next to the Trinity Alps and know that there are epic views out there, but only seeing a wall of smoke.

I've gotten to meet a few different hotshot crews along the trail (forest firefighters), but on the way here there was a big group that had made a meadow alongside the trail their base and I got to watch a few helicopters land and drop off a new crew and some supplies.

There was talk on the trail of an "alternate" route from the top of the ridge down the big 2000 ft descent in Seiad Valley that took a forest road instead of the trail. This alternate was off the map and unsanctioned, but supposedly shadier, with more water, a bit shorter, and much more gradual of a descent as it followed the creek into town.

So, I cheated. Well, I don't know if that's the right word, but after taking a bit of heckling from some other hikers for taking the road instead of the trail ("You know, if you walk a bit further that way, you'll get to I-5, and that takes you all the way to Mexico") I set off on a side adventure. Because I've decided that's what this is after all, right? An adventure. And sure the road walk was a bit easier, and scenic, but it turns out I have absolutely no willpower. About 4 miles down the road I passed a family packing up their car after their swim in the creek, and with NO PROMPTING FROM ME (promise!) they offered me a ride into town. Which I couldn't turn down. So on the way in to town I got to hear all about the town drama and how everybody in town grows pot.

Now the downside to taking the road into town was that I now had to camp in town, instead of a couple miles outside of town on the trail. And the RV park charges hikers an arm and a leg (well, $15) to camp on their lawn, and I heard the proprietor wasn't the friendliest towards hikers. So, another hiker (Two Tone) and I camped under the bridge leaving town in a homey little hobo campsite and stayed up super late (y'know, like 9:30p) talking. It was like a slumber party!

Seiad Valley Cafe is the main attraction in the town, and was featured on the Food Network for their infamous "Five Pound Challenge." The challenge is to eat a pizza tray stacked with 5 one pound pancakes, with the accompanying stick of butter and cup of syrup, in two hours. Many hikers along the trail talk about their attempts on the challenge, but I hear from the lady who runs the cafe that she's only had two people finish it in seven years. I was a little pancaked out from the allyoucaneat pancakes

Sunset through the smoke near Donomore Creek, just after crossing into California.

Helicopters bring in a new crew of firefighters and some supplies, near Bear Dog Springs in California.

Here you can see "the seal of the great state of Jefferson." And no, that's not the cafe, that's the bathroom.

115

at Callahans, so I settled for a nice breakfast burrito and a highly recommended German chocolate cake milkshake.

I had planned on grabbing breakfast, picking up my resupply package, and hitting the trail early, but it turns out the post office doesn't open til noon so I'm stuck here until at least noon. Looking around here in town, I keep seeing this funny symbol with two "X"s, and reference to "the state of Jefferson," so of course I had to Google that (wiki article). Turns out the region here comprised of southern Oregon and Northern California has been trying since about the 1940s to become its own state, called the State of Jefferson, and they're very serious about it. Everything here bears the symbol of "the seal of the great state of Jefferson." Feels very confederate. They're also fighting very hard to keep the area south of the Klamath from becoming a national monument.

"Nor cal" in thru hiker speak is the area between Sierra City and the Oregon border, much different than the definition of nor cal I'm used to that means "north of Bakersfield." I thought there wasn't much up here, but I'm finding that nor cal is pretty crazy! For example, in the town of Belden, every weekend is a huge rave or giant festival or something that people pay hundreds of dollars to attend, but hikers get in free. And that's all that that town is. During the week it's just a sleepy community.

Highlights from the last stretch:

Passing "The Ravens" – a family of four, kids aged 8 and 11, hiking the whole PCT. I love seeing families with kids out on the trail, because it proves having kids doesn't have to mean you have to stop having adventures! I love telling those stories to people I meet who say they can't do certain things "because they have kids now." Check out their amazing blog: https://theravens15.wordpress.com/

And some more great signs:

Award for best sign of the week: *Someone was having fun with their units here…"25,000 mm"?*

Award for coolest historical sign: *So weird that we're hiking on an old wagon trail!*

rejected by the klamath. and awkward (?) questions.

august 11, 2015

Okay, first things first – it's been a while since I handed out an improvised gear award, and this one comes to us courtesy of "The Duchesse." So out here, it's difficult to get clean – the dirt really embeds itself in your skin, and who really carries a bona fide washcloth? Being fed up with the inability to exfoliate properly on the trail almost led The Duchesse to pack a loofah, until she realized she could WAD UP HER MOSQUITO HEADNET and accomplish the same thing. Brilliant!

Y'all can blow your minds with this last batch of pics: https://flic.kr/s/aHski4BysY

Now, encouraged by my adventurous entrance into Seiad Valley (the off map forest road + hitch), I was curious to try another adventure leaving town. Either you can walk for 6 miles on roads way out of the way to the nearest bridge and back, or ford the Klamath and cut off four of those miles. At least one northbounder told me it was totally doable and only a couple feet deep, so I walked across the field outside of town, took off my pants and shoes, and started wading. The north half of the river was super easy, but I spent almost an hour looking for a route across the second half, and a way up the steep south bank. Finally I gave up, waded back to my start, and cut myself up climbing the bank full of blackberry bushes. After which I still had the 6-mile road walk. I guess not all adventures are successful 😫

Which is a nice segue to my next adventure. So the trail is a place where questions that in any other situation might be awkward, become totally (?) normal. Such as

In some places, this is about the best scenery you get. Gotta use your imagination to fill it in. ▼

It is absolutely CRAZY the amount of force water has. Along Grider Creek (which was beautiful!) there are a couple places where the bridges have been demolished.

I've finally gotten my mind wrapped around the idea of WATER coming from the ground, and then they "spring" this on me?? Scott Creek nuthin', they should call this Keystone Light Creek. Break time!

"bro, can you tell me if my back has a rash?" (shouted from across the creek as he's removing his shirt) or, more recently "hey, can you drain my blister on my foot?"

Okay, let me explain. I had stopped to eat dinner because it was the last water source before camp and people had congregated there. This gentleman and I had kind of connected because we were both southbound, but I guess it just took him a little while to get the courage to ask me. He waited until I had packed up and put on my backpack to leave, and then explained that because he was older, he wasn't flexible enough to reach around the back of his foot and drain this huge blister. So that's how I drained someone else's blister for the first time.

Now, as far as scenery, I would LOVE to get you guys some great pics, as this stretch from Seiad to Castella passes through some amazing huge vistas in the Klamath and Shasta-Trinity National Forests. But the smoke has been as thick as fog since about the first of August. So this is definitely a stretch I plan on repeating when California is not on fire (if that ever happens, lol. I'm surprised there's any forest left up here.) If you wanna join me, chime in below in the comments and I'll let you know when I plan it ☺ Check out a report on some of the fires here: http://www.nasa.gov/image-feature/goddard/series-of-wildfires-in-northern-california-continue-blazing

Sorry, this post is a bit scatterbrained, but another resource if you can't get enough talk of life on the PCT is a travel blog called "Halfway Anywhere" and he's compiled a list of his posts from when he did the PCT. His style is very thoughtful and funny, and less descriptive storytelling: http://www.halfwayanywhere.com/pacific-crest-trail/

A couple of my favorites:

- http://www.halfwayanywhere.com/trails/pacific-crest-trail/say-yes-almost-everything/

- http://www.halfwayanywhere.com/trails/pacific-crest-trail/hate-hiking-love-adventuring/

- http://www.halfwayanywhere.com/trails/pacific-crest-trail/what-its-really-like-on-the-pct/

- http://www.halfwayanywhere.com/trails/pacific-crest-trail/thru-hiker-superiority-complex/

The middle of Marble Mountain Wilderness is an odd place to have a comments/suggestions box. But don't worry, we hikers hijacked the notebook inside and turned it into a trail register.

We hikers are a lazy bunch. If we're gonna hike 4/10 of a mile off trail for water (probably down a hill) we wanna know if there's gonna be water when we get there. This guy tried to be helpful, but I saw this note on 8/6/15 – see the problem there?

Satellite image showing the wildfires (red dots) in the Shasty-Trinity and Klamath National Forest areas, and all the smoke sweeping east across NorCal.

Well that's it for now. This next stretch takes me across the valley, past Shasta and over to Lassen. Gonna be dry, and there's a 30 mile water carry, ugh.

Time for some good signs:

Most Encouraging *(only 999 to Canada!)*

Most Useless *(good thing someone out here likes doing puzzles – these are the people you have to be worried about when you shred your documents)*

Most Confusing *(so, can I not drink the water later when I get into the campground? Top sign says don't drink, bottom says it's the campground water supply...)*

natural and man-made wonders

august 21, 2015

Random song that's been stuck in my head for the better part of the last stretch: "8 Days A Week" by the Beatles. On repeat. It's getting pretty old.

And, those of you who know me know I hate the heat. I thought I was escaping it this summer by fleeing to the mountains, but it has followed me. It is rapidly draining my motivation.....but never fear, I have found a way to beat the heat! This brings me to my first "natural wonder" of the post: the subway caves! They're lava tubes and they're dark and like 45° F inside, so I'm sitting inside them writing this post while I cool down. I really wish I had brought my air mattress down here, you better believe I'd be taking a nap.

So yeah, I really wasn't actually looking forward to this past stretch of the trail that crosses NorCal from Castella to Old Station. There weren't a lot of landmarks I was looking forward to, and it was gonna be a hot dry slog. So, the theme of this post is "natural and man made wonders" (as you might have already guessed from the

The lava tubes are accessed through areas where the roofs have collapsed. But don't worry, the rest of the length of the cave should be fairly structurally sound. Except that place halfway through where they point out that it partially collapsed.

I've never seen NorCal from this perspective before, it's so easy to get tunnel vision on an interstate. Shasta on the right, Castle Crags on the left. I-5 goes up through a valley on the left half of the photo. Just remember next time you head north past Redding and Yreka, you're driving through THIS.

See that? Right there? Okay, really I'm just having fun making annotations on pictures with my phone. But that really is Shasta. And the smoke really did clear for a day.

title), wherein I point out all the amazing things I saw and pondered in a seemingly barren stretch.

First amazing thing that happened was that the smoke finally cleared, and I got my first "peak" of Mt. Shasta (zing!). Followed by many more views from all different directions, including a panorama with both Castle Crags and Shasta.

I keep thinking that surely I've passed all the north-bounders by now, and I resign myself to a lonely day. And still, I keep passing them! Many of them have found a renewed enthusiasm after passing the midpoint in

Impromptu party at Ash Camp, on the McCloud River!

The bathroom at Ash Camp. This was very foreboding…definitely the most suspenseful "nature break" I've taken this entire trip. On the flip side, I think this would make a great band name – "May Be Bats."

Let's play a "Where's Waldo" game. Who can find the water source here? This was a very important spot, as it was the only water for like 12 miles in either direction. Answer below.

Yup, right there. A puddle about the size of a dinner plate, and an inch deep. But it was a MAGIC puddle, no matter how much water you scooped out of it, it didn't get any smaller.

Chester, CA. I can't imagine what it's like for them to have been hiking longer than me, and not even be out of California yet! Side note: the best question I've gotten from a northbounder is "what's the halfway point for you southbounders? (Me: um, Chester I think?) Oh, that's right, I guess it's the same for both of us…"

Two days out of Castella, after much tromping past rampant poison oak and my first swimable (is that a word?) and laundry-able (okay, that's DEFINITELY not a word) creek in quite a while and after seeing my third bear for this trip, I popped on into a forest service campground on the trail for the night, and found a group of three fly fishers who invited me over for a beer. And as I hung out, northbounders started trickling in…one by one…until there was quite a crowd and we had drunk all the fishers' beers. We were regaled by stories of the pair of northbounders who had been antagonized by a mountain lion for an entire night, and stories of one of the fly fishers' dads who had been a bodyguard for the Cuban president before the current regime.

After plenty of forest walking, it was time to head out on to the ridge for the rest of the way down into Burney Falls. But not before the water situation started to get pretty annoying. At this point the water report is getting a little old so northbounders were telling me that some of the springs ahead were dry. Oh well, it'll be practice for the upcoming 30 mile dry stretch at Hat Creek Rim ☼

So heading into Burney Falls I passed another couple of-wonders, these ones man-made. I've passed under lots of power lines by now, but for some reason there was a set that seemed particularly intriguing, so I stopped and had

These are the power lines of which I speak. Perhaps they look unimpressive, but they were, in fact, very impressive.

So cool…and pretty!

"first lunch" next to them, and listened to them crackle and hum. One thing that was so interesting was that of all the towers I could see supporting the lines, there were at least three different styles. Why were they different? And how much time and investment went into laying hundreds of miles of high voltage line, cutting down a wide swath of trees on rugged mountainous terrain and placing huge trussed metal towers every hundred yards or so? If the lines went down, how many thousands of people would be without power?

Shortly after, I came to Britton Dam, and was mesmerized by the water flowing from the turbine outlet. The shape of the dam overflow was so beautiful too – a mathematically perfect curve to maintain laminar flow of the water until it hit the flow diverters/spoilers at the bottom, presumably to minimize bank erosion downstream with a sudden influx of high velocity water. So much planning and thought went into this dam…into each PART of this dam. Think of the turbine alone – the rotor was mathematically designed, then cast from refined ore, the ball bearings on which it spins at thousands of RPM are a technological marvel in and of themselves, the copper windings that it turns in the middle of a huge magnet.

But I didn't stop for too long…I could hear the Burney Falls General Store calling me with cries of ice cream. Which, by the way, is universally the thing that hikers want in town. Because despite all our technology, that's one thing we can't get on the trail – freezing cold ice cream. So, I continued on in to Burney Falls, expecting a po-dunk little campground inside a dry and dusty state park. But oh my. Oh my indeed. This brings to my next wonder, a NATURAL wonder. Burney Falls is the single most wondrous natural phenomena on the trail so far.

"Upstream" less than a mile on Burney Creek is a dry creek bed. Nuthin'. But at the falls the water has cut away the ground down past the water table, and so not only does surface water spring up before the falls and go over, water is coming out of the face of the falls too – 100 million gallons a day. And in the valley the river has made, the air is so cold because this is all ice cold groundwater.

So after seeing that, I went and had my ice cream. Made possible by Britton Dam and compressors and refrigerant.

To my dismay, I learned that there were not, in fact, laundry facilities at Burney Falls State Park as I was led to believe. But there were pay showers, so I bought a bar of soap and a travel-size bottle of shampoo and got sooo clean (side note: the formulation chemist in me KNOWS that they're both "just soap" but for some reason they both work so differently! Ever try washing your hair with bar soap?). Then used the shampoo as laundry detergent and washed my clothes in the sink (surprisingly difficult to do when the sinks don't have a stopper). I was desperate….last time this shirt was washed was Ashland, and future opportunities may be few and far between.

Then, after sleeping in and being generally lazy (my excuse was that I had to wait until the store opened so I could donate my leftover soaps to the hiker box…) I set off towards the infamous Hat Creek Rim – a hot, exposed, 30 mile waterless stretch.

But even that! Even that was not without wonders. Just

Less than a mile upstream of the falls, bone dry. This is Burney Creek. Wait for it…….

ohgoshwow. eyegasms. Look and be amazed.

So good it merited two pictures. I never would have expected to find this in the middle of ugly NorCal (no offense NorCal).

out of Burney Falls was the single most amazing cache/trail magic/trail hangout spot. So it's AFTER the dry stretch for the northbounders, but BEFORE for me. So for me it was like eating dessert before dinner. But wow!

A fully stocked kitchen cupboard??!

And a kitchen area??!

And a recharging station??! Do the wonders never cease? (Sorry, you don't get to see a pic of me using the solar shower.)

There was a cooler with sodas and water (and I'm told beer, for the first hour or so after they stock it, lol) that were STILL COLD, there was a solar shower, a camp stove, lanterns, a solar phone charging station, and a kitchen cupboard stocked with food. Oh, and chairs…. oooooh chairs. Lemme tell you, it's hard to leave a place like that.

Up up and away onto Hat Creek Rim. My mileage didn't work out such that I could make it through in one day, so I'd be dry camping about halfway through. But Forest Road 22 brought two more wonders: wings and water. There were tons of hang gliders and parasailers flying around, maybe twenty, and I was so distracted I almost didn't see the water cache just off to the side. People who build (and more amazingly, maintain) these things blow my mind.

So I'm definitely gonna get to a point here. Noticing all these natural and man-made wonders brought to mind what's sometimes referred to as the watchmaker analogy: when many people see a natural wonder, they think "Wow! It's amazing that all this came about stochastically, through millions of years of random chance, and all these parts happen to work in harmony." But not a single person would think that about about a dam they came across…or power lines…or a water cache. Those clearly were made for a purpose, by intelligent beings, and yet the levels of complexity of most man made wonders are arguably nowhere NEAR as complex as natural wonders. I believe it takes more faith to believe that natural wonders are a result of random chance than that they were created by God.

Hope I didn't lose ya there. But yes, I made it through the stretch and into Old Station, and realized an

Now THIS…THIS is gourmet food. Eaten in style.

So this is embarassing. I actually had to ASK someone which mountain was Lassen. The other volcanoes have been so obvious, and well, "peaky." But when Lassen blew its top, it REALLY blew its top. So it's not that tall anymore, and really just a huge crater.

And then the more useful of the two wonders. People! I mean water, definitely water. Look at all those gallon jugs!

Camping up on Hat Creek Rim also meant I got to see a pretty spectacular sunset. And stars! Don't see too many of those in the forest.

UN-wonderful thing. Post offices aren't open on Sundays. And today is Sunday. Which is why I'm sitting in a cave writing a blog post instead of unpacking my resupply box. But! That also gave me time to go to JJ's Diner and eat the most amazing 1/2 lb burger and four large cinnamon rolls. So, you know, I guess it's okay 🍔

Next stretch takes me (hopefully!) into some trees, and I hear there's plenty of ups and downs (including a 4000 ft climb out of Belden? Sheesh!). And the midpoint! And a few intermediate stops I'm looking forward to – I'll let you know how they turn out 🙂

Ah, I'm almost shivering now. This is perfect. Now if only there were wifi down here…

If you're hankering for more, check out the rest of the pics from this stretch here: https://flic.kr/s/aHskixFG-mG

Also, I found some other random cool stuff, that I tacked onto the end of this post.

Is that a bird? A plane? An artificially flying human? But seriously, there must be dozens up there. DOZENS!

So I've seen plenty of siamese trees before. But here's a tree that grew around another dead tree!

I honestly, seriously, don't know what to make of this sign. Would this be a good band name? OR WAIT NO a good trail name!

This might be the most delicious thing ever. I'm gonna call it "trail pizza" even though it hardly even bears a vague resemblance to actual pizza. Humus, pepperoni, mustard, and mayonnaise. (Yes, mayonnaise, which I have decided is the nectar of gods. And yes, this is the only time you'll ever hear me say that.)

my sidetrip to sierra city to conquer the gutbuster: a photoessay

august 26, 2015

Okay, okay, I know what you're all thinking. "A photoessay? But we love the pages and pages of rambling that normally come with Toddalicious posts, and the pictures are always boring."

Don't worry, there will be pointless commentary to go along with the pictures. It'll be like a storybook. For grownups. Because it's about mountains and food. And mountains of food.

So we've established that, apart from the awful dry stretches of southern Oregon and northern California where the trail talk is always about water, everywhere else the trail talk is primarily about food. And so it was that as far north as Washington I heard legends of a 1-lb burger that was delicious and only $9.99 in the small town of Sierra City, whose second claim to fame was as the gateway to the Sierras on the PCT. What could be better than a gigantic burger to kick off my walk through the Sierras, and celebrate the end to this monotonous NorCal? Answer: nothing. So without further ado, some pictures.

So our story starts here. What does a beautiful panorama have to do with a burger you ask? It was as I looked out over this landscape that I realized I was getting into the Sierras. Also my GPS told me the same thing. And the Sierras mean Sierra City. And Sierra City means "the Gutbuster."

I'm told these are called the Sierra Butts. Wait, let me double check that. Ah, the Sierra BUTTES. Regardless, we're definitely in the region where things start having Sierra in their name.

Slowly getting closer to the Butts. When you're walking, you have MUCH longer for the anticipation to build. I'm trying to give you that same sense. You're welcome.

So I inadvertently got to see the sunrise up on the ridge. I was hurrying to get to the next water source for camp, since I didn't have enough for the night, and made my first navigational error! I accidentally almost climbed the Sierra Butts instead of going around them. I blame the trail...my "exit" was not clearly marked. It definitely wasn't me being distracted by the promise of a burger.

And here's the backside of the Butts the next morning. Does that mean they're mooning us? Dang, should've gotten a pic of them with the moon over them. That'd be like a picture pun. Guess I better hike back there and try again.

So normally these signboards on the trail are reserved for notices like "Total Fire Ban" or "No Camping Naked Next 5 Miles." But you can tell Sierra City has their priorities straight!

Aaaaaaand the PCT literally just dumps you out onto Hwy 49. "Go west, young (hungry) man!"

The moment we've all been waiting for! Okay feet, you know what to do. You're "Plan B."

And thumb, you know what your job is too. Loud and proud...you're "Plan A."

A magical transportation device appears! Good job, thumb. Your reward will be to help me ingest the burger. John was nice enough to give me a ride into Sierra City in his beautiful red Prius.

Sure, I could've dragged out the story a little longer, but here's what we're all waiting for. The guy making it was "Grandpa" and was holding his baby grandchild as he prepared my behemoth. I'm not sure what the Health Department says about that, but I didn't mind. Also, the fact that it was packaged "to go" might have been a subtle hint to not be a typical hiker and loiter, but I DID NOT take that hint.

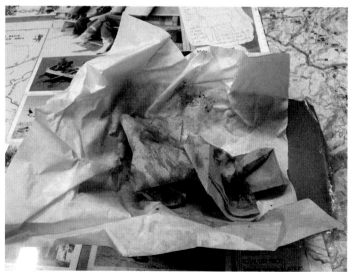

Proof that I won the battle. If you want to see what the inside of the burger looks like, you'll have to come here yourself (do it!).

So since Sierra City wasn't one of my "re supply stops" on my "schedule," I "had" to head out back on the trail right afterwards. But not half a mile down the trail I found this – the Yuba River – in all its glory. Doesn't matter if you've already "wasted" most of the day in town, you just can't pass up a swimming spot like this. Oh man. Yup, didn't get many miles in today. Oh well 😆

So that's the story, folks. Now you'll notice in that last caption a few of the words are in "quotes"…like "schedule" and "wasted." It's taken me a while, but these words are meaning less and less to me. Or, no, not meaning less, but their meanings are changing. Schedules are still important, but you have to evaluate the reason behind them. And wasting time is bad, but what constitutes a waste is changing. Check out this song by Chris Rice that's been going through my head, called "Life Means So Much": http://youtu.be/ciYQmlh4Xe4

catching up!

september 2, 2015

Okay, I'm slacking – it's been a long time since I updated you guys, so lets have story time. I'm gonna try something here, and it's gonna require your help. Out here on the trail I don't have access to fancy tools like Adobe Illustrator, or even MS Paint (shudder), so what I'm gonna do is give you guys a picture of where I'm at currently and I need you to imagine your best classic "flashback water ripples" on it (you know, like they have in movies and stuff, to take you back in time).

Here I am now…time to flash back.

Have you done it? Okay, great. The date is August 17, 2015, and I've just picked up my resupply package from the local itty bitty post office in Old Station with the annoyingly limited hours (11a-3p, M-F) and vowed to start using local stores instead of post offices when possible to hold my resupply packages. Wondering what a resupply looks like? Here's mine, as received in a large flat rate box:

So neat and tidy! And well tetris'd in there! My mom is a pro!

And after a bit of unpacking, it gets sorted into breakfast, lunch, dinner, and snack ziplocs, then thrown into a big food stuff sack. I seem to carry much more food than other thru hikers, and I'm still trying to figure out why.

So yeah. Food was all set, and it was time to head out. In the middle of the day…it was sooo hot. But as I told you last time, there were a couple things this stretch to look forward to. First off was Lassen Volcanic National Park, and shortly after entering that was a place that I'd heard glowing reviews of from nearly every hiker – the Drakesbad Guest Ranch. It's what my family used to call a "dude ranch" where people have family reunions and there are activities like crafts, archery, horseback riding, and a hotspring-fed pool. They have quite the dining room too apparently, and they let the hikers "clean up" the buffet for half price after all the guests have eaten, and hikers can use the other facilities too! I'm a sucker for a breakfast buffet, so I timed my schedule to show up at 8:30a sharp, and was rewarded with the most beautiful plate of French toast, eggs, and sausage I've ever seen and homemade berry sauce. Then, being the only hiker that day, proceeded to clean out the breakfast buffet. And then finish off the rest of their extra French toast. As I waited for my 3000 calories of breakfast to settle, I got to watch and talk to one of the guests who had gotten out her spinning wheel. She was spinning yarn to knit a sweater. Talk about going back to basics!

But alas, the life of a hiker is on the trail, so I said goodbye and hit the dirt. So far Lassen NP had been pretty mundane, but the map promised the "Boiling Lake" and "Terminal Geyser" as side attractions. The Boiling Lake

Here it is, ready to go!

133

Boiling lake.....oooh scary!

was a nasty looking steaming and bubbling brown soup of a lake, and Terminal Geyser was not a geyser but a steam vent. I'll put forth here that I'm not super impressed with the NATURAL features of Lassen NP, but I would go back for Drakesbad 👍

Next up was the town of Chester. Chester was allegedly home to one of the trail's best trail angels I was excited to meet, and a well-rated milkshake shop. But when I got to the highway into Chester, I decided to pass on since it was a bit late in the evening to go into town and I didn't really need anything. But I did hang out at the trailhead long enough to drink an ice cold ginger ale from the ice

I've spent hours thinking of an interesting pose to do while I took my selfie, and this is what I ended up with. I'm so boring.

chest there 🍺

The next day, just a few miles south of Chester was the official halfway point of the trail. The marker is very nondescript and I almost walked right by it.

Oh gosh. And then Belden. Where do I begin? Belden is in a ravine, right along the North Fork of the Feather River. It has a history related to the old gold miners which they try and showcase, but really it's just a festival destination where they have music festivals and parties and raves every weekend.

It's so interesting – about half the hikers I encountered told me "whatever you do, MAKE SURE you get to Belden on a weekend!" while the other half insisted exactly the opposite – "whatever you do, MAKE SURE YOU AVOID Belden on the weekend!" Apparently many hikers get vortexed into the raves there and have to spend a few days detoxing and recovering before they can get back out on the trail. Whatever – I had an average burger there on a Thursday afternoon, served to me by what appeared to be some burned out druggies and procrastinated as long as possible before having to get back on trail and climb out of the ravine.

Next stop after Belden was Quincy, and a resupply. I heard from a hiker on my way that Quincy, being the county seat, had a building across from the courthouse called the "Crisis Intervention and Resource Center." They provided counseling and help to victims, and services to the homeless. What that meant for me was a free shower and laundry!

The other major milestone that happened in Quincy is I finally retired my water bottle. After 1300 miles of squeeze filtering all my water, it finally sprung a leak.

Belden is so cute and homey, right? Right??

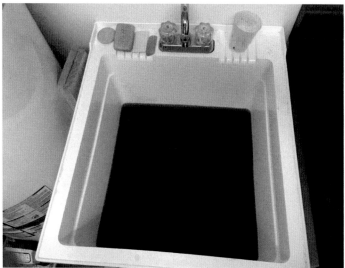

This is why I always have to "prewash" my clothes. This is a water rinse of just my socks and pants!

What this tells me is the disposable bottle I got when I paid $2 for overpriced water was waaaaay overbuilt.

After Quincy was the milestone we've all been waiting for – Sierra City! (You HAVE been waiting for Sierra City with me, haven't you?) Sierra City is the official un-official start of the Sierras, and home of "the Gutbuster." One other thing I noticed in Sierra City – tiny general stores on the trail may not have a huge selection of regular items, but they have exactly what hikers want.

Finally I rolled into (or rather, walked into) the I-80 rest stop late in the evening to grab some water with the plan of continuing on another couple miles. But we all know how that goes…I ended up spending the night camping at the rest stop. Bathrooms? Water faucets? Picnic

In best Toy Story alien voice "farewell my friends, I go on to a better place!"

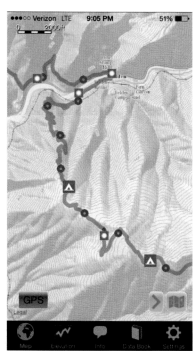

This climb is NO JOKE. 4000 ft straight up!

Milk? No, we don't have that. But we do have EVERY BRAND YOU CAN IMAGINE of fuel canisters for backpacking stoves!

135

Side note: here's how the PCT crosses under I-80. It feels so... stealth.

Cold Springs is the best piped spring on the trail!! You just walk up and hold your bottle under the flow. Kind of feels weird leaving the "faucet" running though as I walk away.

tables?? Can't leave that.

Well, actually, there was another reason I couldn't leave the rest stop. So I had been trying to stay strictly on schedule because I had planned a family meet-up in Truckee, just east of the I-80 crossing. The plan was to push through to Tahoe since I was passing by Truckee on a weekday, then family would get me from Tahoe and have a blissful weekend in Truckee. But reality got in the way. I've gotten this far without serious foot problems (well, except for the first week...that was pretty awful) but for some odd reason a few days before I-80 I got some crazy blisters on the bottoms of my feet and walking on them gave me bruises on the bottoms of my feet. So...I swallowed my pride and asked dad if he could pick me up a couple days early on his way into Truckee. I spent the next day being a complete bum at the rest stop, and then spent the next FIVE DAYS being a bum in Truckee, sitting on the couch with my feet up.

But that's a story for the next post ☺

On the right I've tabulated some "regular" highlights from this last stretch.

I found this sign south of Lassen NP really funny. I'm used to signs saying that motorized vehicles aren't allowed on the trail, but are hang gliders that common of a transportation device that they have to be expressly prohibited?

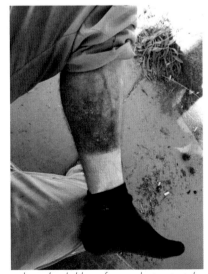

This is what my legs look like after a dusty stretch...even with long pants! Can you tell where my sock line is?

And now, some FOOD highlights:

I never got into the whole Top Ramen thing in college. I guess now's my chance.

Mom likes taking chances and throwing wild cards in my resupply box. This week's was bacon bits, so I was trying to figure out how to use them. Bacon and chocolate go together, right? How about bacon bits and Nutella? Combined with the regular peanut butter and dried bananas?

PHEW! Hey look at that, we're back at present day! And I'll catch you up on the side trip to Truckee in a bit!

it's hardly desolate out there...

september 15, 2015

Yup, whenever I look down at my feet now I think I'm wearing clown shoes. DMFG ("doesn't matter, feels good." These must be hedonist shoes.)

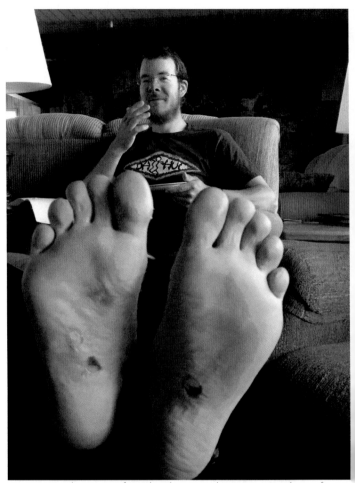

Here's me showing of my battle wounds as I eat a plate of cookies dad brought me. It's okay, though, because I'm still smiling.

Okay, first off, my new shoes are AWESOME. My first time in Altras, and they're the Olympus model. You know, those shoes with the soles that are so thick they look silly? Yeah, well it feels like I'm walking on pillows, so there.

Now a heads-up – I'm not really a very emotional guy, but this post might get a little mushy, so any softies may want to leave the room (just kidding, don't leave). But we will return to our regularly scheduled seriousness with the next installment, I promise.

So I mentioned before that I had a plan to meet up with family in Truckee, but I was going to be hitting Truckee in the middle of the week. My dad and stepmom had already moved around their schedules to come up to Truckee mid-week before I was able to get cell service to tell them I'd hike on through to Tahoe where they could more easily pick me up on Friday. Despite my repeated

And my stepmom, not to be outdone by dad's plate of cookies, got me a foot bath. How could I NOT be smiling?

Sorry, no pictures of us actually USING the kayaks…my phone's too precious to take in the water.

RIDING A BIKE IS SO FAST! AND YOU CAN COAST DOWN HILLS! Thanks for the great ride Chuck, Megan, and Emily 😀

And here's a destination that's been on my list for a while: Fallen Leaf Lake. Made better by the presence of a canine companion!

Here's Chuck showing us he's got what it takes to eat like a thru hiker: avocado, hamburger patty, and almond butter on cold sourdough.

insistence that I'd be fine pushing through to Tahoe, they continued to plan for a midweek arrival in Truckee. More than once they said, "are you SURE you don't want us to grab you mid-week on our way through?" "No, no, I'll be fine," I repeated confidently.

And then reality happened. After 1500 miles of no debilitating foot problems, both my feet decided to blister up right under my arches. And then pushing through two more long days earned me some bruises because of those blisters. So it was that I limped into the I-80 rest stop. Can I do 65 more miles like this? Do I really want to? And so I called up Dad. "Dad? You know how I was so confident I could push through to South Lake Tahoe? Well…can you pick me up on your way to Truckee tomorrow?"

And you know what I got? No I-told-you-so, no "good

The PCT and the TRT run concurrently for a bit. These are like… the two best placards…in the same place!! A perfect match 😊

Fontanillis Lake was incredibly beautiful, would definitely come back here to camp and swim.

And the view from the top of Dick's Pass at 9400 ft – highest point so far on the trail! Here you can see Middle and Upper Velma Lakes, Fontanillis Lake, and Dick's Lake.

Aaaannnddd the view looking the other direction from Dick's Pass.

thing we took these days off." Just a knowing, "sure, just hang out at the rest stop and we'll be there tomorrow." And then all that weekend they were so thoughtful and went to the drugstore to get antibiotic ointment, foot powder, and Epsom salts. And my sister brought me my new pair of shoes 👞

My family is awesome.

And what a great weekend of friends and family! Kayaking, bike riding, board games and card games, and some great food! Gotta say, after five days of that it's hard to break away.

But I was really looking forward to Desolation Wilderness! So breakaway I did.

Desolation Wilderness has seemed special for a long time – my aunt and uncle took me and my dad on long backpack trips there a few times, and Lake Aloha was one of my uncle's favorite places to be. I didn't think I'd be passing very close to Lake Aloha, though, until I checked my maps the day I was set to hike through Desolation. At that point the anticipation started building and I was looking forward to it all day.

All of the lakes in Desolation were beautiful, and I was expecting more of the same from Aloha. It was so long ago I couldn't remember it specifically, but at the end of the day when I crossed over the northwest ridge it absolutely blew my mind. It was stunning! And it was exactly the kind of place my uncle would love…bare majestic granite peaks of the Crystal Range towering over a flat lake with lots of granite islands dotting it. It feels like you're on the top of the world.

For those who don't know, my uncle, one of the most amazing people I know, passed away last year from cancer. And walking along the shoreline of Lake Aloha for that mile and a half I got all teary-eyed. I knew that even though it was early in the evening, my day was over and that's where I was camping.

So, my charge to everyone out there, is to explore the world and find a place that's so "you" that it will remind people of you long after you're gone. A place where they can go to feel your presence. A place that you love to be. And then share that place with people.

And my charge to the parents out there: let your kids find that place. I know we're crazy and we stress you out, but thank you for letting us take risks, and make mistakes, and then still love us. Thank you for supporting us. I can think of at least a few parents who are doing a great job raising some adventurous kids (yes, we're still kids!): Roger and Dorothy Shimer, Dan and Ramona Slagel, and of course my parents. I can't tell you how many times I've called up my mom, not to ask for permission, but to tell her about my next crazy adventure. Thank you all so much.

Coming up over the ridge on the northeast side of Lake Aloha, all of a sudden the sky just opens up around you and you're on a granite plateau filled with a lake and islands. It's absolutely impossible to properly photograph, but I sure tried.

Sunrise on the Crystal Range after a pretty windy night.

And kids (anyone with parents, really): cherish and appreciate your parents. And let them know it.

All the pictures in this post (and more!) available here:
https://flic.kr/s/aHskjLC4WF

the long stretch, pt. 1: "when the cold wind blows it chills ya, chills ya to the bone."

september 16, 2015

I'm headed towards THIS?? Hmm…maybe my days of good weather are over…

So, for those of you who got the reference in the title, props. For those who didn't, your homework is to watch more muppets movies (Yes, sometimes you have to do things you don't like. It's for a good cause.) This was promised to me by my route planner to be my longest stretch (in terms of days), and even though it wasn't (cause it thinks I'm a slow poke) enough happened to have to split it in two.

Anyways, two days after Truckee brought me to Echo Lake, and after downing a quick milkshake from the Echo Lake Chalet (duh!) I hitched a ride into South

Lake Tahoe to pick up my resupply and eat as much pizza as I could stuff in my face at the Round Table near the store that had my package. So the store holding my package was a small outdoor shop called "Lake of the Sky Outfitters" and they love the hikers. While I was hanging out in their hiker lounge, the salesperson called on my help a few times with customers to offer my opinion as the "resident hiking expert" lol. Sure did have fun talking gear for a while 😀

After packing up my food (which overflowed from my bear canister into my extra food bag, don't tell the park

Perhaps not the most ICONIC view of the ride, but this is the trailhead at the top of Carson Pass, where participants of the infamous Death Ride get an ice cream after completing their fifth summit of the day.

143

Crossing over the ridge after Carson Pass I saw this. And I can't caption it what came into my head, as surprisingly that includes a few profanities. And I'm trying to keep this blog PG. But suffice it to say I was impressed.

rangers), I caught a ride with a local back to the trail. I had some brand new motivation, as I was about to head into a section of the Sierras that really felt like home, including Emigrant Wilderness and Sonora Pass.

You know how I've been complaining about the heat for the past, well, forever? Well, right about this time a frigid cold front made its way down from Alaska (so I'm told) and brought with it the most ferocious and incessant wind I think I've ever experienced (except maybe for that one time at Tongariro). For two days and two nights it was just staggeringly windy, 60-70+ mph winds in places I'm sure (though I'm no human anemometer) but it was pretty fun. It also brought some cool clouds to make my pictures pretty.

And the trail took me some places that some of you may recognize, that certainly brought back memories for me.

After crossing Carson and Ebbett's Pass was Sonora Pass, and a sudden dramatic shift in the landscape. But the night before summiting Sonora Pass I finally got "caught" by a southbound hiker named Waldo. He was really clocking the miles – he'd started July 9. Waldo is about my age, and is already a triple crowner (he's done all three of the major trails: AT, CDT, and PCT) and this was his second time doing the PCT because he was "looking for something to do this summer" while applying for grad school. I got to hike with him for about two days, and he makes now two southbounders who have started after me and passed me.

Those of you who know me know I'm prone to making really bad analogies. So I'm gonna start including bad analogies in each post. I'm like the family member on a long car trip who keeps passing gas, but you just have to put up with it because there's nothing you can do. So as long as I'm in the "car" of your family and friends on

Here is view of Alpine County, home of Markleeville and the Death Ride.

And what would any hike be without suggestive geographic features named after body parts? This was referred to affectionately as "the nipple," and was indeed quite suggestive from both sides. You can see it was a very cold day.

the "road trip" of your life, you'll have to put up with my flatulence (I mean bad analogies). But also with my flatulence unfortunately. So that's this week's bad analogy.

I've converted a bunch of photons into pixels for you, which you can convert back into photons at your convenience here (note that some of these are going to be included in the next post): https://flic.kr/s/aHskkjs6g9

the long stretch, pt. 2: really, people? no stoves?

september 25, 2015

So after camping a few miles north of Sonora Pass and waking up with frozen water bottles (hey, at least my reconstituted milk for breakfast was ice cold!) I headed towards the alien landscape of Sonora Pass – the mountains were rapidly changing from the forested granite I'm used to, to this expansive barren world of massive brown and craggy peaks. Now, of course, the trail never takes the easiest route over the passes, so first it takes us up to 10,500 ft to look out OVER Sonora Pass, and then descend down to it.

There are some amazing people in the world, and I'm continually interested to hear how everyone has a story, and often one you would never guess. Walking towards Leavitt Peak in this crazy area I passed a girl on the trail with a bunch of tattoos and piercings, and with a small dog whose head was poking out of her backpack. She is apparently (she claims) one of only five people in the world to run more than a hundred 100 mile running races, and she's only in her mid thirties I'm guessing.

On my way south of Sonora Pass, I met a weekend backpacker, but I didn't get a chance to really talk to him until after we'd leap-frogged a few times. Then we hiked together for a few hours and it turns out we're both nerds – he has a chemistry degree and is doing an internship with the USGS in the Bay Area. We had some great conversations about Radiolab and xkcd, and lamented the fact that advanced mathematics classes are prioritized in the academic curriculum over statistics and logics classes.

But seriously, guys, the area just south of Sonora Pass looks like you're walking on the moon. If you ever get a chance, come check it out.

It was really hard to believe that somehow, this weird, brown, landscape was going to transform into Yosemite National Park soon. Like really soon. But right before my eyes, it happened!

Alas, despite the beautiful welcoming party of Dorothy Lake (side note, guys – it's not a good idea to go for a swim in a frigid lake shortly before dusk. Pretty sure I almost hypothermia'd myself...) the first 40 miles of

Ever seen Sonora Pass from above?

Descending to the pass, all the creeks and springs were frozen. Watch your step, it's slippery!

And fortuitously, it was at this time, when I happened to have a hiking companion, that I passed the 1000 miles to go marker! Can you tell how stoked I am?

Have you ever seen Hwy 108 from this perspective? It winds past Gianelli Cabin, the Dardanelles, and Kennedy Meadows in this giant valley.

Yosemite were no "walk in the park" (zing!). As I'd been warned, all the canyons in Yosemite run east/west, so walking north/south through the park means walking down into and then up out of a series of huge canyons. Definitely did some soul searching during my many unplanned breaks in the heat and smoke that had resurfaced to make the switchbacks even more not fun.

But, that only lasted a couple days, and crossing Benson Pass gave me some new motivation! I was pushing through the end of a long day, looking for an excuse to cut it short, when such an excuse miraculously appeared.

I was walking past a creek as the daylight faded, and an older gentleman stopped me and asked "If I had some information."

Me: "Um, what kind of information?"

Him: "Do you know where it is?"

Me: "Where what is?"

Him: "The, um, the junction."

Me: "What junction?"

And of course this pic doesn't do it justice, but this is the view after coming up a ridge headed south from Sonora Pass and looking through the notch.

Him: "You know, the, um, three way. What's it called. I don't remember."

Me: "The next junction is in three miles..."

Him: "That's too far. I gotta get out of here."

Me: "You okay? I think the most direct way out is on the PCT, and that's 23 miles."

Him: "I've been out here too long and I'm losing my mind. I gotta get out of here."

Me: "You got enough food?"

Him: "Ummmm...(long pause)...just barely."

And just like that, I'd found a friend to camp with for the night and a way to ditch my extra food, lol. Robert was a retired pharmaceutical chemist doing a 550 mile stretch from Dunsmuir to Vermillion Valley Resort, at the age of 71. And apparently he has quite the following in Medford, Oregon, due to his adventurous exploits. Unfortunately though, his ankles were giving out on him, and he didn't have enough cold weather gear for the cold evenings that were starting to come in for the autumn. I tried to give him some of my dinners, but he didn't have a stove!! So I just gave him all my bars.

The next morning I made sure he knew where he was headed and had enough food, then headed out. A few miles down the trail I could swear I smelled bacon cooking. Impossible! I thought...who packs in bacon? And

You think our govt built a big wall to keep immigrants out, look how big a wall mother nature built to keep people out of Yosemite!

then I saw it...a huge full trail kitchen set up, with horses tied up nearby, and I was hailed by the cook to come in and have a sausage and cheese bagel. What trail magic!! All I had to do was answer the typical thru hiker questions from all the people present on the pack trip and I got TWO sausage and cheese bagels!

So I heard from a lot of northbounders towards the beginning of my trip that you run into a lot of people along the trail that you thought you'd never see again. And I was like, "yeah, right. Probably only if you're a northbounder." But it really is wild when it happens. I said hello to hiker at a lake I passed, and introduced myself. She said..."wait, Shade? I've met a Shade before. At a lava field...in Oregon." Well that's weirdly specific,

A bit smoky, but still good views!

The meadows in Yosemite are so soft, they get rutted and then hikers make new trails next to them. In some places I saw as many as five parallel trails! But that's too mundane of an explanation. I prefer to think that Yosemite is on the forefront of hiker trail technology and is implementing multi-lane trails to handle all the increased traffic. Including a middle "turn lane" for trail junctions.

The best kind of magic...trail magic!!

I thought. And then I said, "wait! Are you the person who I gave my extra toilet paper to at the lava field just outside Sisters??" And indeed it was. And because of this odd connection, I felt comfortable enough to ask if she had any Chapstick I could borrow because my lips were killing me. All she had was some tinted Burt's Bee's "Shimmer Lips," but I was desperate, so I took it.

And let me tell you, it was amazing. I felt like a diva ALL DAY. Oh, and I guess it made my lips feel better too.

Speaking of running into people you don't expect, when I got into Tuolumne Meadows I met up with Sailor again. And a guy named Chuckwagon, who I'd heard all about from a girl named Captain Squares up in Callahans. Chuckwagon was in the process of finishing off a fifth of whiskey all by himself in one day when I got into the campground about 4 pm. And he was successful by nightfall...got some more stories there, you can ask me about them in person some time 😊 That night we all camped in what we hoped was the hiker/biker campsite, but I'm pretty sure was actually just a flat patch of ground behind the restrooms. I guess I need to start getting into camp earlier so I can actually find the proper campsite.

But yeah, I'm meeting more and more people going stoveless – meeting Robert makes five. I've decided going stoveless is the trail equivalent of being a vegetarian. How, you ask? The answer is today's bad analogy! (said in best Alex Trebek "Daily Double" voice)

Being stoveless is like being vegetarian – both voluntarily limit their available food options, both love explaining to you how their diet is just as satisfying as yours (when it isn't) and both have a choice to face in filling the void left in their diet. Some vegetarians avoid meat in their diet but then try and replace it with imitations (fake meat? Soy "bacon"?), while others just choose alternate foods. In the same way, no-stovers can either try and imitate hot food by just soaking regular dehydrated meals for about an hour and then eating it cold, or just eating things like sandwiches that don't need cooking.

I don't think I could do stoveless. I do cold breakfasts and lunches, and never heat water for coffee or tea, but there's just something about a hot dinner that just nourishes the soul. Do you think you could?

Here's one of those vegetarian ironies I'm talking about. Grabbed this from the hiker box on a stretch where I was woefully short on snacks.

well, it's finally happening

september 25, 2015

Now just TRY and tell me you could pass up a place like this to camp…

Hang onto your hats, boys and girls, this one's a long one. The theme song for this post is "Disconnected" by 5 Seconds of Summer (https://vimeo.com/89796612), because it's been so darn difficult to get any connectivity between South Lake Tahoe and Tehachapi! There are some good pics here in the post, but as usual (and in fact more so because of the amazing scenery of the High Sierras) there are more beautiful pics over here in the full Flickr album for this section: https://flic.kr/s/aHskm6EeaF

So after hanging out with Sailor and Chuckwagon at Tuolumne Meadows, I took off bright and early the next morning. Ha! I'm just kidding. I never get out of town early…I left at like noon, after eating two breakfasts from the Tuolumne store grill and finishing off about half a package of dehydrated eggs (about 6 eggs) from another hiker. Leaving Tuolumne meadows has you hiking along the Lyell Fork of the Tuolumne River for a while, as it meanders along a nice flat meadow before going up and over Donahue Pass and leaving the park.

A couple fun things happened before the pass: I met Daybreaker, a 76 year old guy doing the entire PCT in one season (!), and I had rangers on horseback check my bear canister. I was really happy at that point to be a law abiding citizen, but I had to stand awkwardly by as the person I was walking with (who did NOT have one) was given a huuuge guilt trip by the ranger. Apparently they couldn't issue a ticket, though, since we weren't technically "camping" at the moment. STILL haven't been asked for my thru hiker permit.

Anyway, on the way out I passed Sailor, and we decided to head most of the way up the pass together but make

151

Just before the sunlight hit the mountains, looking north to Yosemite from Donahue Pass.

it a short day and camp at this wonderful glacier melt lake in a huge basin. It was such a treat sitting in camp at 5pm, listening to the rumblings of rock and ice falls far away on the distant mountain side.

The next morning was up and over Donahue Pass, which I feel is like the gateway to the remote sections of the Sierras – sections I've never seen before such as the Ansel Adams and John Muir wildernesses, and Sequoia and Kings Canyon. This would also be home to the highest passes in the Sierras – we would go over 7 passes above 11,000 ft, and the highest point on the trail (Forester Pass) at 13,200 ft. We left going south with some trepidation, however, as we had heard lots of reports of absolutely awful smoke from the Rough Fire filling the mountains, obscuring the views and making it difficult to breath. Lots of JMTers (John Muir Trail hikers) were canceling their trips, and at least one southbound PCTer had cancelled his.

Fortunately the smoke didn't start out too bad – we'd have every day until about 2pm before it would blow in. So that first day we got to see some epic views of the Ansel Adams wilderness, Thousand Island Lake (omg so beautiful!), and we pushed it all the way til just past Red's Meadow, by Mammoth Lakes.

This promised to be a fun and beautiful stretch for other reasons, too – this section of the trail runs concurrently with the John Muir Trail for about 200 miles, and is believed by many to be the most beautiful and most strenuous stretch of the PCT. So we would have lots of company from all the JMT hikers. Sure was fun getting to hear their different perspectives…although we're both on the same "trail," we have different equipment, different goals, different speeds. And they're all so clean! And their gear doesn't look all worn out like ours!

Which leads me to the point where I explain the title of this post. I'd gotten so far I thought maybe I was going to make it all the way…but I think when you're thru hiking it's inevitable that your equipment starts getting worn out. And not just the consumables. When I was having lunch just north of Mammoth, I found out the makeshift frame I'd DIY'ed for my backpack had finally broken after about 2100 miles and 5 months of daily use. As luck would have it, I had a brief period of cell service there and I popped online and ordered a new

Thousand Island Lake was incredible! It definitely tied with Rae Lakes for my favorite lake of the stretch.

I "accidentally" took the Devil's Postpile alternate and got an up close and personal view of these cool basaltic columns.

152

backpack to be delivered to my upcoming resupply in Independence. Shortly after THAT, (and I'd seen this one coming) my trekking pole tip fell out because it was completely worn through, so I was mono-poling it for the last 100 miles into Independence as well. So that brings my list of worn out gear to:

- 1 pair Darn Tough socks (which was happily replaced for free!)
- 2 pairs NON Darn Tough socks
- 1 backpack
- 1 set trekking pole tips
- 2 pairs shoes
- 1 Smart Water bottle

Sailor and I had been bumping into each other all down the trail, but we'd never really hiked with each other. From Tuolumne, though, our schedules and goals lined up and we decided we made a good team so we started crushing miles together. At the top of each pass, we'd joke that while some people are "peak baggers," PCT hikers are "pass baggers," and we'd add another notch to our belt of passes.

Resupply in the High Sierras is a bit tricky. Either you have to hike quite a ways off trail and over a high pass, or be willing to pay exorbitant prices to have a pack station pack it in and hold it for you. Or both. To break up the long stretch between Tuolumne Meadows, we both opted to head into the least expensive of the High Sierra resort options, Vermillion Valley Resort, and then hike out over Kearsarge Pass and into Independence. I wasn't too sad to skip Red's Meadow, but we heard story after story about how amazing and awesome Muir Trail Ranch was,

This is literally THE ONLY TIME I have been "asked" to loiter. And you don't have to ask me twice.

The whole resort is run off of a generator, and has no wifi or landline phone service, but gosh darn it they gotta have Dish Network! Those JMTers need their sports fix. So cool at night when the generator shuts down at 9:30 and the whole resort goes instantly dark.

and were bummed not to at least have stopped in for a meal and soak in the hot springs, or grabbed some food from the overflowing hiker box.

Since the beginning of the trip, I had been looking forward to Vermillion Valley Resort. Not sure why, maybe because the name sounds pretty, or exotic? Guess that shows you the power of a name – I knew literally nothing about the place. Anyway, I heard a lot of north-bounders complaining about it, telling me to avoid it if possible. "The lake's dry," "it's super expensive," "they take stuff out of the hiker box and resell it," "it's just a fishing camp." I looked long and hard at my schedule, but there was no convenient way for me to avoid it. And boy, I'm glad I didn't avoid it.

VVR might be my favorite resupply point yet, which is saying something. Yeah, the lake's dry, yeah, it's expensive. But you can tell when a trail stop loves the hikers, and VVR loves the hikers. When you first walk in, the owner lets you grab a free drink out of the fridge (beer, cider, or otherwise), and every night they have a hiker campfire.

One reason people love the High Sierras is because of how remote they are. VVR is hours away from town on a tiny one lane dirt road. I had been counting on at least A LITTLE connectivity at VVR to let my aunt know I was on schedule for our meetup in Independence, and to ask my mom to bring a few things. But because of how remote it is, there's no cell coverage, and wifi costs $8/hr for about the speed of dialup. When I asked if they had a pay phone, the guy kind of chuckled and said, "we're

So here we are, walking "through" Lake Edison. I'm actually gonna call it Edison Meadow.

off the grid here, we have a satellite phone, for $2/min."
I was told there was a little bit of AT&T coverage if I
walked out onto the lakebed. But I'm learning out here
in the Sierras that not being able to connect takes a huge
load off of my mind. I don't feel "obligated" to upload
stuff, to contact people, because it's simply out of my
hands.

But the downside to VVR is that it is a HUGE hassle to
get to from the trail. There used to be an (expensive) ferry
that would take you across the lake, but that was back
when there was a lake. Before I continue, let me clarify.

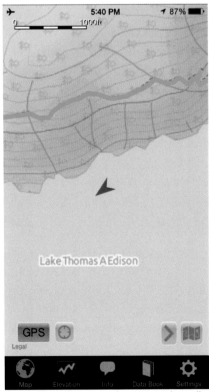

Look at that, a modern day miracle. We're literally walking IN THE LAKE.

VVR sits on Lake Edison, which is a reservoir made
and owned by the Edison Power Company, but it's been
getting lower and lower over the past few years and right
now it's at 13% capacity. So basically it's a meadow with
a puddle in the middle. So now, the option to take a ferry
still exists, but you have to walk an additional half mile
down the lakebed to the shore, then the ferry picks you
up, and then on the other side they drive you the rest of
the way to the resort. The other option is to walk, either
across the lakebed or on a trail, each one about 5 miles.
The process is repeated to leave the resort, although they
will shuttle you to a nearby trailhead that provides an
alternate (though no shorter) hike out to the PCT.

Shortly after VVR the smoke got pretty bad, and stopped
clearing at night to give us beautiful mornings as it had
been. It really feels like the smoke is a monster that's
been chasing us down the trail.

Regardless, this was home to one of my favorite stretches
of the trail. Through Kings Canyon area, after Muir Pass,
there's a canyon you walk through, and thankfully the
smoke wasn't quite thick enough to obscure the walls of
the canyon. Along the top of the west edge of the canyon
was a series of distinct domes and I could just imagine
I was walking along a corridor in Egypt with a row of
huge stone pharaohs looking over me. I have no idea if
this has anything to do with the park being called "Kings
Canyon," but I will always think of that canyon as the
"Valley of the Kings."

We also learned from the owner at VVR that Mexico,
not to be outdone by the storm front that had just come
down from Alaska, was sending up its own storm front
that was gonna hit in about four days, so we boogied as

And here you can see where the water level has been in past years.

154

See those mountains there in the distance? Yeah me neither. In a way it was kinda cool, because it felt really otherworldly and eery. But in another way it kinda wasn't cool, you know in the way where it burns your nose and eyes.

fast as we could down to Independence. I'll tell you about that in the next installment 🌩

Oh! And don't think you're getting away this time without a bad analogy. I've decided choosing a campsite for the night is like dating, with the goal of finding a spouse. Think about it – in life, as on the trail, you can only go forward (no backtracking to a previous campsite) and you never know if the campsite you're passing now is the best one you'll find for the evening, or if the next one will be even better. But unlike dating, you get to repeat the process every night, so the stakes aren't QUITE as high 😉 I'm such a campsite player, I spend the night with a different one every night.

I don't know if this peak has a name (and frankly I couldn't be bothered to check), but I'm going to call it "God's Thumb." Seriously, it's definitely a giant thumb. [Editor's note: For those curious, this is "properly" known as Fin Dome.]

OH MY GOSH THE WORLD IS CROOKED. Or wait, maybe just the camera is. This was the second self-timer attempt, the first time the camera fell of my backpack and gave me a beautiful blurry pic of the ground.

Lake McDermand, on the way to Muir Pass.

155

So I'm skeptical about what makes a spot on the trail in the high Sierras a "pass." Seems like they just cut switchbacks up a wall of rock wherever they want. Side note, maybe this is where they got the inspiration for Lombard St. in San Francisco. (on the way to Mather Pass)

Confusing Sign of the Section Award

"Meadow On Rotation Schedule." I guess we got to see the meadow that was currently working the swing shift. A quick googling shows that quite a few hikers take pictures of this sign and no one seems to know what it means.

Best Trail Sculpture Award

It was a...ROCK LOBSTER! Well, a rock monster anyway, but there aren't any B-52's lyrics about rock monster trail sculptures so I had to improvise.

Rae Lakes tied with Thousand Island Lake for "best lake in the High Sierras," and it was especially cool because of the low clouds that had replaced the smoke. I recommend this as a place to hike into from Onion Valley.

Wanda Lake, just south of Muir Pass.

View looking north from Mather Pass. I guess we're a "little" ways above the tree line.

Ascending Palisades Creek on the way to Mather Pass. Looking back west into smoky Le Conte Canyon.

Here's Sailor, being a trouble maker and contemplating the best way to wreak havoc on the suspension bridge over Wood Creek.

lean on me

september 27, 2015

So the theme of this post is about how much better life is with relationships, and how important supporting each other is. The song that's been going through my head is "Lean On Me" by Bill Withers (http://youtu.be/4Qz-pSeDsHIw), so listen to that before you read the rest of this post and get in the right mood ☺

Oh, and have I told you how awesome umbrellas are? No? Well then let me just say it now, for the first time, lol (for those of you new here on the blog, it isn't the first time).

We left off last post with a weather front coming in as Sailor and I raced to get over Kearsarge Pass (11,760 ft). Apparently we made quite an impression on one of the JMTers we passed named Proud Feet, because a few days later on the trail after our stopover in Independence, someone asked us if we were the two guys they had heard about who had been "running" to beat the storm. Anyway, just before Glen Pass, the smoke was exchanged for clouds, and visibility dropped to about a hundred feet. We had a bit of rain heading up from Rae Lakes to the top of the pass, but you better believe I was prepared with my umbrella. This made Glen Pass really surreal and unnerving, as it is literally a knife edge on top, and it looked like we were descending into nothingness on the other side.

We had only a slight drizzle the whole way up Kearsarge, but it rained pretty solidly on us the whole way down to Onion Valley, the trailhead where we would catch a ride into Independence. As luck would have it, we caught

See both of those trees "leaning" on neighboring trees? That's my attempt at being clever and sticking with the theme.

Looking down through Onion Valley to the Owens Valley.

And the best view from a pass yet. Looking west from Kearsarge Pass.

two day hikers just finishing up and didn't even have to wait for a ride into town! The only "downside" was that we had to share the back of their hollowed out van with their two dogs for the long windy road into town. We assured them that was not a problem.

In town we discovered that Independence has zero services. No restaurants to speak of, no grocery store, just two gas stations and a Subway. But we had made it! We could see the nasty clouds hanging out over the mountains, and we would hear stories from other hikers for the whole next week of the snow that fell on Bishop Pass that night, how some people got hailed on coming over Kearsarge, how everything above 11,000 ft got a dusting of snow, and how some people were holed up in their tents for 17 hours waiting for the storm to pass! Instead we were cozy in a motel room eating ice cream and taking showers.

So it really is great hiking with a partner. When strategizing mileage and resupplies, two heads is better than one, and Sailor is great at some aspects of planning that I neglect (like asking about the weather forecast!). It's also great for motivation, and makes the days go by faster. And I usually have extra food and sometimes he's a bit short so he helps me lighten my food load 😉 After a quick survey of the available lodging options in Independence, we found the Mt. Williamson Motel and Base Camp, which advertises itself as hiker friendly. They weren't lying!

So, before I continue, you need to know about the "thru hiker superiority complex." But on top of that I'm going to add the "SOUTHBOUND thru hiker superiority complex." You see, thru hikers kind of get this sense of superiority because they tend to get special treatment and lots of oohs and aahs. But southbounders, when we come through, often get even more special attention because there are so few of us. The shop owners get excited because they get to deal with us one on one, instead of in huge crowds, and they can give us little special perks sometimes.

Such was the case at the Mt. Williamson Motel and Base Camp. We checked in, and not only did the office have the most well organized and stocked hiker box, the office clerk gave us a couple free beers and offered to do our laundry for free (normally $15!). After we had gotten all cleaned up and made a run to the convenience store, we made friends with the hiker staying next door. She was hiking the JMT with her dad, but he had already gone to sleep, so we were just hanging out on the lawn

Hey look at that! A rare snow patch sighting just under Forester Pass!

talking until late. With Sailor being a licensed therapist, the conversation got pretty deep pretty fast. The office clerk dropped by with another couple free beers "for a nightcap" and asked us if we wanted anything from the convenience store since he was heading over. We didn't need anything, but on his way back, he dropped off a bag of potato chips.

Looking south through the notch that is Forester Pass. Hard to believe we're at 13,200 feet.

So I can't tell if the office clerk was this nice to everyone, or just Sailor and me, for some reason? We kept joking with our JMT hiker friend about it, because SHE hadn't received any of these special "perks," and even when we were all hanging out together on the lawn, all the clerk's questions were addressed to just Sailor and me. Regardless, would definitely recommend this place. Just make sure and be a male southbound thru hiker I guess? Lol.

The next morning, after we got our packages from the post office, we all three hitched into Lone Pine for food and a couple camping supplies. We were lured into the barber shop, however, and both of us guys lost all of our hair. My mom and my aunt arrived to meet me just as I was finishing up my haircut, and they joined us for some milkshakes and gave us all a ride back into Independence.

I was so excited to see my mom and aunt! So waaaay back at the beginning, before my trip, within about a week of sending out my proposed schedule, my aunt had asked me if she could please drive out to Independence to resupply me. This was in addition to meeting me at Cascade Locks, and potentially at Tahoe or Tuolumne. The High Sierras are near and dear to her heart, and I think she was just as excited to see me there and be able to talk with me about everything I'd been seeing. I am so blessed to have family that comes out to support me, and puts up with the difficulty of planning an exact meetup date!

The three of us (my mom, my aunt, and I) headed back up to the Onion Valley campground to have a wonderful evening camping (for a change, lol!). I believe if you want the most out of your experience meeting up with a thru hiker, you have to camp with them. Mom provided the chili and cornbread and steamed broccoli, and my aunt pulled out her maps of the Sierras with all the routes drawn on it of all the trips she and my uncle had taken and all the remote lakes they'd backpacked into, and we just talked about the Sierras, now that I've gained a bit more respect for what they are and have spent (a bit) more time in them. And oh what a luxury it was camping with them in a huge four person tent! By far the best night of camping on the whole trip. Felt like a slumber party 😊

My family is awesome.

The next morning they sent me off with a big breakfast and an appropriate number of hugs (i.e. A LOT) and I set out for Forester Pass, with my sights on Mt. Whitney

At the Whitney Portal/Trail Crest junction everyone ditches their packs for the final push to the top. They…that's right, they "lean" their packs against the rock. See me struggling to stay on theme here? Anyway, it's like a small city of backpacks.

Zoom way in here and you'll see a long line of people on their way to the summit. I count at least 14 (see inset below). This is definitely one the things that loses its impact when photographed.

the next day. Going back over Kearsarge Pass I got to see the amazing views I hadn't on my way out because of the clouds, and it was spectacular.

That day I got just past one of those silly Sierra passes where it seems like they just picked any old point on a ridiculously high ridge and just carved switchbacks up to it, since there's no obvious low point. This silly pass happened to be Forester Pass, the official highest point on the trail at 13,200 ft.

Summiting Whitney was cool, but I think far less cool than doing it from the eastern side. From the western side, you can't even see it until you're literally on top of it, and it doesn't really feel like a big accomplishment because it's "just a day hike." The trail to the top is like a little highway.

So after Whitney, we had a small powwow and realized that for the next 62 miles there were only three water sources. Just like that, we were leaving the Sierras and heading into desert.

So I always thought the Kennedy Meadows on Hwy 108 was the only Kennedy Meadows. But people raised in SoCal apparently have always thought THEIR Kennedy Meadows was the only Kennedy Meadows. Anyway, now I've seen both. Kennedy Meadows (south) is a charming place, and Scott is the most helpful proprietor.

And then, a day after Kennedy Meadows, we were really in the desert.

Thanks to all the amazing people who stock water caches in that barren wasteland, we successfully navigated the

Maybe this is another reason why it doesn't feel like a huge achievement to summit. They brought a WHOLE HOUSE TO THE TOP. Surely that's more difficult than bringing myself to the top....

I think I need to explain this one. There were no less than FOUR different survey markers in the rocks on the top. I guess they were all double checking each other and stuff. You know, "leaning" on each other.

Kennedy Meadow's guide book on backpacking equipment could probably use a little updating though.

Here Sailor does battle with a marmot that desperately wants his food.

And you can tell they try really hard to keep up with current trends at Kennedy Meadows (south).

"driest stretch of the PCT" between Walker Pass and Tehachapi.

So this week I've got a really great bad analogy for you: thru hikers are like people that listen to commercials on the radio. Weekend backpackers buy an album and listen to the whole thing, day hikers buy singles on iTunes, but thru hikers listen to one radio station continuously, commercials and all. Of course what I mean by that is that we don't pick and choose the best parts, but rather take the good with the bad, boring with interesting. And I think experiencing nature this way is really insightful for two reasons: one, because you get to see regions transition into other regions (like the Sierras and Mt. Whitney transitioning into the desert), and two, because when you see how much monotonous space there is between truly amazing points on the trail, you gain a new appreciation for how truly unique and amazing the unique and amazing parts are. When all you see is the best parts, it's easy to believe that "it's all like that" and it seems a bit less unique.

The award for most creative sign goes to this one, just outside Kennedy Meadows (south). I guess they didn't have any numbers in their character set? And as I think about it more, these aren't even transparent letters...they specifically made a backwards "P" instead of a nine. Odd.

The day after Whitney we were seeing scenery like this.

Waking up well before sunrise to hike amongst cactus and Joshua trees? Yup, that's the desert.

It probably doesn't have the full impact here, but this gate earns
the award for the "Most Ineffectual Gate." It's intended to keep
bikes and motorcycles and cars out by making pedestrians
walk over a bar, but it only works if there's fence on either side
of it. This was in the middle of nowhere, easily walked around.

an adventure!

october 2, 2015

So here's the LA Aqueduct. I kinda thought it would be open. Also, it's empty. Goes on exactly like this for about 15 miles.

One thing that's stuck with me from my school days is something I heard from one of my teachers, and the idea is this: if you're taking a test and you don't know the answer, you end up writing an awful lot more than necessary, trying to make up for quality by increasing quantity. Those who know the answer can answer concisely, and don't need to disguise their lack of understanding in theatrics.

I think that's relevant to life in so many ways. Lately I haven't really known what to include in my blog posts, I don't feel very insightful, so I'm just kind of making them these long descriptive lists of things I did and people I saw, and it's gotten to be just a routine – hike a section, write about it, repeat. But I want to break the monotony

and talk just about an interesting adventure yesterday, and since I KNOW what I want to write about this time, maybe it'll be more interesting 😊

I heard lots of stories about the desert from the north-bounders, so I thought I was "prepared" for it. But I had no idea how fast it would run up and smack me in the face! I've gotten used to the slow pace of California, where everything takes hundreds and hundreds of miles to change since it's so long. After Whitney everything is coming so fast – one day past Whitney, after close to a month in the Sierras, I'm out of the Sierras. Two days past Whitney and I'm in the desert. Less than a week past Whitney I hit the driest stretch of the entire trail – the stretch where everyone had told me about the 44

Look at all those shade trees! Okay, I'm being sarcastic. But there were probably AT LEAST two shade trees for this past 40 mile stretch of desert. In fact, one of the waypoints on my map was for "Large shade tree, 50 yards off trail." No joke.

THIS is what beauty looks like in the desert. No, not Sailor, the water jugs.

165

mile water carry – only it had been exacerbated because the two "reliable" springs that bookend that stretch are dry, so it's a 61 mile stretch between natural water sources. I am incredibly thankful to the people near the trail who stock the water caches in this area of trail and turn it from an impossible stretch to just a difficult one.

Yesterday, after a well-deserved zero day in Tehachapi catching up on phone time for the first time in weeks, I called up one of the numerous people who had given me their phone number for a ride to the trail and got started again. Seriously, as I had sat at Starbucks that day, no fewer than four people gave me their phone numbers in case I needed a ride.

Which brings me to my adventure. There are three things I've avoided on principle this whole trip: hiking with headphones, hiking at night, and getting a 40.

Yesterday I got my 40. Which was necessarily accompanied by the other two things.

It was a spur of the moment decision. I had planned on a regular distance day, but when I got to the aqueduct at the end of the day and realized it would be a flat road walk with no shade for the next 17 miles, I decided it would be much better to hike by the light of the (fortuitously full) moon than to do it in the heat of the day with no water tomorrow. I had loaded up on podcasts and an audiobook in Tehachapi because I knew I had a few more days of desert, and I blew through all of them, then half of my music library. There's something so freeing about throwing your plans and norms to the wind and just being a bit wild.

It was also perfect because right at the 40-mile mark was a trail angel stop, dubbed "Hiker Town," where I could stay and wash up. So I'm writing this now amidst clucking chickens in a weird little place that is built to look like an old west town. And I got to separately shampoo and condition my beard. Tell me that isn't the high life right there.

One of the podcasts I listened to was an interview with someone who I thought was a random person, but turned out to be the drummer from Jimmy Eat World. Apparently he has a side project with his wife, and I can't believe the coincidence, but the band's name is "The Wretched Desert." I kid you not. Check out one of their songs: http://youtu.be/u02on2aBro8

There are at least two other songs running through my head right now, one about Lancaster and one about Palmdale, but I can't link them, because they're not really audience appropriate ☹

Maybe I'll be out of the wretched desert soon. BRB gotta go do some more road walking, ugh.

let's be honest

october 3, 2015

Okay, the windmills were pretty cool. At least I can include one pretty pic here.

Let's be honest. At Tehachapi, I ceased to be a hiker, and instead became a bum with a credit card. I'm no longer enjoying multi-day stretches of beautiful scenery and drinking water from cascading streams or springs. This is no longer as much of a nature adventure as it is a logistical nightmare.

Maybe I'm being a bit extreme here, but it feels like I'm beating my head against a brick wall. Sure, the trail has had its ups and down (literally and figuratively of course) and I've had bad days and good days, and I DO believe that part of the trail is about overcoming obstacles and pushing through tough times. But this feels different.

For the 200 miles since Tehachapi, I've had occasion to use my water filter all of about one time. Every water source has been a ranger station, or a fire station, or a campground spigot, or a town restaurant. I haven't had to dig a hole to "do my business" in weeks because I pass actual outhouses a few times a day. As the trail wanders through the "Pleasant Ridge Wilderness" in the Angeles National Forest, it crosses Highway 2 no less than nine times. Maybe I can chalk all that up to the fact that I'm hiking next to one of the largest metropolitan areas in the world.

But then there are the burn areas. Southern California is becoming one continuous burn scar, requiring endless detouring and rerouting. If it didn't annoy me so much from a practical standpoint, I could step back and see how depressing it is. Many of these are well established detour routes and only require some road walking or

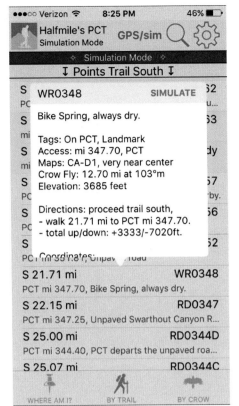

Screenshot 1:

●●○○ Verizon 📶 8:25 PM 46% 🔋

Halfmile's PCT
Simulation Mode GPS/sim 🔍 ⚙️

◇ Simulation Mode ◇

↓ Points Trail South ↓

S WR0348   SIMULATE

Bike Spring, always dry.

Tags: On PCT, Landmark
Access: mi 347.70, PCT
Maps: CA-D1, very near center
Crow Fly: 12.70 mi at 103°m
Elevation: 3685 feet

Directions: proceed trail south,
- walk 21.71 mi to PCT mi 347.70.
- total up/down: +3333/-7020ft.

Coordinates:

S 21.71 mi   WR0348
PCT mi 347.70, Bike Spring, always dry.

S 22.15 mi   RD0347
PCT mi 347.25, Unpaved Swarthout Canyon R...

S 25.00 mi   RD0344D
PCT mi 344.40, PCT departs the unpaved roa...

S 25.07 mi   RD0344C

WHERE AM I?   BY TRAIL   BY CROW

I think my PCT app is teasing me. Why would it list a water source, only to tell me it's "always dry"?

Screenshot 2:

●●○○ Verizon 📶 8:28 PM 45% 🔋

Halfmile's PCT
Simulation Mode GPS/sim 🔍 ⚙️

◇ Simulation Mode ◇

↓ Points Trail South ↓

S 31.34 mi   PL0338
PCT mi 338.06, PCT follows an unpaved road f...

S RD0330   SIMULATE

Paved road to a water tank. No access to water.

Tags: On PCT, Paved Road
Access: mi 329.79, PCT
Maps: CA-C14, center-ish
Crow Fly: 20.45 mi at 094°m
Elevation: 3532 feet

Directions: proceed trail south,
- walk 39.61 mi to PCT mi 329.79.
- total up/down: +6842/-10683ft.

PCT mi 330.06, National Forest boundary

S 39.61 mi   RD0330
PCT mi 329.79, Paved road to a water tank. N...

S 40.16 mi   PL0329
PCT mi 329.25, High voltage power line.

S 40.37 mi   RD0329B

WHERE AM I?   BY TRAIL   BY CROW

Hey look! There's a water tank over there! Oh, no, you can't actually have any of the water.

Screenshot 3:

●●○○ Verizon 📶 8:28 PM 45% 🔋

Halfmile's PCT
Simulation Mode GPS/sim 🔍 ⚙️

◇ Simulation Mode ◇

↓ Points Trail South ↓

PCT mi 342.82, Small wooden hiker bridge

S 27.13 mi   RD0342
PCT mi 342.28, Unpaved road

S 27.40 mi   Hwy15
PCT mi 342.00, WATER ALERT: Next northbou...

S 27.53 mi   TR0342
PCT mi 341.87, Side trail to McDonalds, mini-...

S 27.54 mi   Cajon Pass Road
PCT mi 341.87 meets the Cajon Pass Road

S 27.87 mi   McDonalds
mi 0.34, Cajon Pass Road

S 28.03 mi   WR0341
PCT mi 341.37, Crowder Canyon, small seaso...

S 28.52 mi   PL0341
PCT mi 340.89, PCT passes under a high volta...

S 28.66 mi   RD0341
PCT mi 340.74, Cross an unpaved road.

S 28.92 mi   PL0340
PCT mi 340.48, High voltage power line

S 28.97 mi   RD0340

WHERE AM I?   BY TRAIL   BY CROW

No joke, one of the waypoints is a "side trail to McDonalds." This is the major water source for the area. Guess I really AM in the wilderness.

hitchhiking. But some have no way to go around or require detailed investigation of topo maps or trail maps to figure out. I spend so much time now in town figuring out which obstacles are coming in the next stretch and how to get around them. I obviously can't hold that against SoCal, because fires are a part of nature. But as if to add insult to injury, the first plant to regrow in some of these burn areas is called "poodle dog bush," a poisonous plant akin to, and allegedly much worse than, poison oak. Even though volunteers have been working for the past four years since the Station Fire to clear the trails in the closure and finally open it this year, there are long stretches (at least 30 miles) where hikers must be continually on guard for poodle dog bush branches hanging

I may have already posted this pic, but it bears repeating. Where there are no trees, the trail is prone to washouts and mudslides. The trail here was in pretty bad condition.

Our friend the poodle dog bush. As a thru hiker, it's drilled into our heads to be scared to death of this stuff. Avoiding it sometimes reminded me of dodging laser beams in a bank heist à la Catherine Zeta-Jones in "Entrapment."

into the trail or in some places blocking the trail still.

But repeatedly skipping large stretches of trail starts to feel really cheap. Am I driving this trail or walking it?

Maybe I can just take more breaks under shade trees as I hike to "cool my jets." Oh wait I can't, because either I'm in the desert where there aren't any trees, or I'm in a burn area where there aren't any trees.

This must be why people hike it northbound. This part of the trail isn't a nature or wilderness experience, so hikers turn it into a social experience, hiking in groups and meeting all the trail angels. This is a very difficult stretch to hike solo.

Well, this is my first negative post. I've always heard if you get really upset, give it a day and reassess. Maybe after taking today off and camping illegally near the freeway I'll feel better tomorrow.

gettin' all sentimental

october 8, 2015

Dam, that's beautiful. I thought the Mojave Forks Dam at the confluence of the Mojave River and Deep Creek was a defunct reservoir because it's dry, but it turns out it's just there for flood control, and smooths out flash floods problematic in the basin. Is it ironic that my largest rain event so far has occurred in the desert?

First of all, check out this video I just found that one of this year's southbounders made of his time in the Sierras: http://youtu.be/YK1bamw2iCk

And if you haven't seen it already, check out this awesome video of "The PCT in 3 Minutes" by Mac the Wizard of HalfwayAnywhere: http://youtu.be/styiDn7YKhE

That second video was one of the ones I watched before the trail, and one that got me hooked. It's so wild to watch these videos, now just 200 miles from the end of the trail, and recognize all the places they show (only without snow!), and be reminded of how far I've come. I guess now is the time that I'm starting to get sentimental. Having been in the desert now for a couple weeks, I've become a bit jaded and have forgotten just how awesome this experience has been. I tend to only remember at any given time the previous few weeks, because it's impossible to keep the whole trail in your consciousness at once. I still remember the day I started in Washington, but all the days I spent in Washington and Oregon and Northern California seem like ages ago, like distant memories of years past. These videos bring my sense of wonder back, and even make me a bit nostalgic for those first few months on the trail.

I also can't help but wonder if I "did it wrong," hiking so fast I was at the front of the pack and never had a "trail family." I certainly did feel constrained by time, being

a southbounder, and that feeling seems justified now that I see Horseshoe Meadows at the southern end of the Sierras just got about 6 inches of snow. Most of the southbounders are about two weeks behind me as I hurry through the miles day after day.

But there's something those videos don't and can't portray, and that's the sheer amount of time involved. Now while that may sound blatantly obvious, the time involved plays a huge role in the experience. It's an undertaking that you can't grasp the scale of until you've been

I think this is my favorite sign so far in SoCal. The odd juxtaposition of a fast-food institution emblazoned on a wooden wilderness hiking sign.

After hours in the desert every day, I start to zone out and have "daymares" (you know, daydreaming nightmares) of randomly tripping and falling into a giant patch of cactus like this.

Let's play a fun new game...is this (a) trail magic, or (b) an illegal trash dump site frequented by the homeless?

at it for months already. Sometimes, just like digging for a needle in a haystack, the sheer amount of sensory input involved makes it difficult to pick out, and remember, and appreciate, the wonderful experiences. So without these incredibly condensed video diaries the memory of the trail is mostly gray with a positive spin, kind of like all the memories got put in a blender and puréed. A meal with all its different courses can be great, but usually that same meal put in a blender isn't the most appetizing. (There's your bad analogy for the day.)

And now, after my soliloquizing, a quick update. I made it from Tehachapi, to Acton, to Wrightwood, to Big Bear, and had all my food stolen by an animal last night at the Whitewater Wildlands Conservancy. So without breakfast this morning I covered the rest of the distance to a trail angel near Cabazon who had plenty of extra hiker food to get me to Idyllwild. But now it's just too darn hot to climb San Jacinto – my body is getting thrashed, alternating every couple days between freezing temps

The stretch of trail that goes through the San Bernardino National Forest from a few miles north of Big Bear to a few miles south of Onyx Summit was some of the best trail scenery in SoCal. Such a shame that a few miles of it burned in the Lake Fire this year, now it looks like this.

I don't know why, after all this time in SoCal, I expected to see trees in a wilderness area like San Gorgonio.

at the tops of the mountains and triple digit heat at the desert passes.

I remember during family vacations growing up, mom would tell us about the "golden foothills" and the "golden hillsides" of the Altamont Pass. At the time I believed her, that is that they were "golden," not simply dry and dead. Regardless of what I believe now (take a guess) I think it's amazing how important perspective is in life. There are some people who find the beauty in everything. And apparently it's those people who appreciate the desert.

I…I would sign my name to the end of the post, but I can't remember my name. I've been in the desert, with no one to give me no pain.

And if you're still reading, check out the thru-hiker's theme song: "Walk" by Kwabs

a break from the serious.

october 8, 2015

I know how awful is it to listen to someone complain. So instead of graveling about how boring the desert is, I thought I'd do something else everyone hates, and make bad jokes about rocks. Yes, rocks. While I probably won't ever be a stand-up comedian, I do enjoy making some jokes from time to time.

One thing I've decided, though, is making puns about rocks is hard. Pumice me you won't be too judgemental.

This is a gneiss rock. Just don't take it for granite, it's an easy mistake to make.

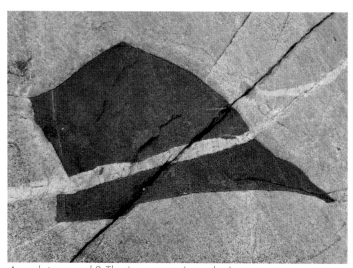

A rock in a rock? That's so meta (morphic).

♪ Shale be coming round the mountain when she comes. ♪

Look at those beautiful white rocky mountain sides. I could marble at them for days.

You can have all the natural caves, but this one's mine.

Hot spring pools are like natural c-rock pots. With people in them.

Volume-wise, in metric this is about 5 liters of rock. In imperial units, it's about 5 quartz.

This kind of rock is like the Wheetabix of metamorphic rocks, because all the grains are smashed flat and packed together. I could get more technical, but that's the schist of it.

If you put your mind to it, I'll bet U2 (that one works because they're a ROCK band) can come up with some rocking good puns. Post em in the comments.

myth and legend on the trail

october 11, 2015

Okay guys, I can't seem to wipe this silly grin off my face. After a day in the mountains with cool air and trees, I'm sitting here in Idyllwild and smiling. I feel re-juvenated and re-freshed and re-ady for some more storytime.

You guys know all those fun acronyms that people use to identify groups of people? Some examples are "mamil" (**m**iddle **a**ged **m**an **i**n **L**ycra) or "dink" (**d**ual **i**ncome, **n**o **k**ids). Recently I was introduced to a new acronym. A hiker I met told me that he was a "myth." A what? I asked. Like, is this guy claiming to be imaginary? Oh, a "**m**ulti **y**ear **t**hru **h**iker" he said.

And speaking of myths on the trail, the human brain sure is interesting. No, it's bigger than that – human NATURE sure is interesting. When our minds aren't feeling completely utilized, we use our imaginations. Our brain is a machine that needs to be always running. So when we're busy with daily tasks and planning and the stresses of society, our brains have no spare processing power and they remain very practical and down to earth. By contrast, out here on the trail, there are very few worries and stresses so the brain looks for things to hope for, to look forward to, to embellish.

To expand on that, it amazes me the small things on trail that become legend. Northbounders were telling me in northern Oregon to sleep at the airport in Tehachapi, something like 1400 miles (two months) back for them. There are some food places that are talked about for hundreds of miles in either direction for their magnificence. By and large these things, when actually encountered, are nowhere near the magnitude one expects from the amount of awe they inspire. I hear of knee-destroying descents, dry stretches that will be impossible to navigate, gross water sources that will make your toes curl. But the truth is our minds want excitement. We want something to look forward to, whether it's a good thing or even if it's a dreadful thing. Our minds want adventure. This is the trail equivalent of gossip – I won't call it actual gossip, because gossip is usually negative, but this trail talk fills a positive role. However, I think its roots in human nature are the very same. I just find it odd that there is very little negativity on the trail.

One of these things of mythic proportions is Fuller Ridge. But, before we continue, a side note. You know how as youths we were all given advice by our elders who wanted us to go into adulthood with a roadmap, knowing as much as they did? And how despite all this, we still needed to have exactly the same experiences they talked to us about before realizing "oh, THAT'S what they meant"? Context is so important for understanding experiences, that advice is often not useful for anyone but the giver. Anyway, I came into Southern California with LOADS of insider information on what to expect, what to avoid, interesting things to see, and it's usually after I've encountered something or passed something that I realize "oh THAT'S what they meant!"

So back to Fuller Ridge. The typical conception of the desert is that it's flat. Most non-hikers think this, and many hikers also do before they get there. But the northbounders told us all, no way! The desert is not flat, it's always either going up or down. This seems like perfectly useful information, right? I mean, we're on the PCT, which goes through mountains. Of course there's ups and downs. But you see, now that I'm here I know what they meant. The mountains in Southern California come in clumps, separated by desert. And there are a number of these clumps. So the trail meanders through some mountains like usual, then drops precipitously down to the desert floor. Then after a bit, climbs straight up to the top of the next clump, and meanders for a bit before reaching the end of that clump and dropping precipitously back down to the desert floor. Ad seemingly infinitum. (or, you know, like 3 times. But it seems like a lot.)

One of these climbs has a particular reputation, and that's Fuller Ridge. Often the climbs happen over a considerable horizontal distance, so the peak isn't visible from the floor; but from the desert floor at I-10 near Cabazon, the trail switchbacks up Mt. San Jacinto, gaining 6500 ft to the ridge that is just 4.3 miles away as the crow flies. The peak is visible the entire climb, and to moderate the ascent, switchbacks increase the trail distance to about 15 miles.

The enormous switchbacks go all the way across the face of the mountain and back, giving you alternating views of San Bernardino on the west face and Palm Springs on the east face. There are jokes that the contractors who made the trail were paid by the mile, instead of by the job. But it, like all ascents, eventually ends (and then climbs another 1300 ft over 8 miles).

I found this abandoned backpack halfway up the climb. He must've gotten fed up with the climb and, well, I dunno.

This is the only stretch in SoCal that has allowed me to suspend my disbelief at the fact that I'm actually hiking past one of the major metropolitan areas in the world.

And brings you into paradise.

The tree cover near Big Bear was nice, but an honorable mention at best. San Jacinto State Park is paradise. When it was triple digits hot down on the desert floor and the Inland Empire area, it was 65°F with a light breeze up top. Huge trees provide constant cover as the trail meanders through huge rocks. If you plopped me here and had me guess where I was, I might say the Sierras. This is like, paradise protected from the encroaching desert by a 6000-ft granite wall. A castle, surrounded by an ironic anti-moat. A king, sitting on a huge granite throne. Okay, maybe I'm being a bit dramatic 😊

And it's hard to believe that in the middle of this is the town of Idyllwild.

Idyllwild is an unincorporated town in the shadow of Mt. San Jacinto. Oh, and apparently the mayor is a dog. There is also a campground in the city, which automatically makes it a winner.

I tried to get out of town around noon, but people kept offering to buy me a drink and hear hiking stories. I'm sure the hiking stories got better the more times this happened 😆

Unfortunately, all good things must come to an end, and in more ways than one. I did have to leave Idyllwild eventually, but the trail south was hit by the Mountain Fire a few years back and is still closed. So the best option is to hitch down to the next road crossing. This is a different Paradise, Paradise Valley Cafe, home to another legend. In cases like these, which require hitches of two

Yay! Trees! Wait...wait...what's that thing right there in the middle?...zoom in, and enhance!

A PORTAPOTTIE?? Yup, in the middle of the wilderness. Must be expensive to deliver and service by helicopter...

different highways, a sign is immensely helpful and I secured a ride in less than ten minutes with a few guys who were headed to that same cafe.

The cafe is known on the trail for its burgers, and I'll admit they are pretty good. But I also get the impression, reading through their hiker register book, that some of this reputation comes from the fact that this is many northbounders' first real burger on the trail…I'm that close to the border! The register is full of enthusiasm from all these fresh northbounders excited to be on their journey, and to them it feels like they've been hiking forever already. I know different. I know Campo is so close. So tonight I'm sleeping on the patio at the cafe so I can have a plate of French toast before starting out. Six days left.

Too bad I can't spend another day in paradise. (don't worry, that link's not a rickroll. But that's exactly what I would say if it WAS a rickroll.)

One of the items I consumed in town was a "weird grilled sammich." It was excellent.

After seeing this sooo many times on the trail, I finally took a picture. Some trees grow in a spiral. I thought when I googled it there'd be an obvious answer why, but there isn't. Intriguing.

scraps

I get lots of time to think on the trail. And now that I'm almost done, there are few thoughts I had that never made it into posts.

While I'm sitting here in Julian eating the free pie, ice cream, and cider they give hikers, I'll list em out for you:

Random Thoughts

- I wonder if Smart Water knows how many people (hikers) buy their water not because of their special vapor distilling, but because of the bottle.

- Blowing snot rockets is much more difficult with unruly facial hair.

- Without fail, when I get a map of a campground, I see what looks like a wifi icon and I get excited. Until I realize it's the icon for an amphitheater.

- Backpacking through these small mountain towns is the best way to see them, because you can go to all the souvenir shops without feeling tempted to buy souvenirs. Instead, I just buy a bunch of good food to remember the town by.

- The desert has the weirdest plants. There's one I swear smells like a cross between new vinyl (you know, inflatable pool toys, not LPs) and bubblegum.

- Making hitching signs is like coloring for adults. Well, homeless adults. Well, homeless "somethings." Am I really an adult?

- I should be conducting a poll on the over/under toilet paper roll orientation debate. I realized on this trip that I'm supremely qualified since I use so many different bathrooms now that I'm homeless.

- When I met some bear hunters on trail it made me think. If I were gonna hunt, it would be cows. Cow meat is delicious, they're usually fenced in, and they wear a bell.

- Dogs would make great backpackers, because they can eat the same food, day after day after day. Their resupply packages would be so simple.

All this fo' frizzle!!

- You know how they make those light bulbs that filter out certain wavelengths so they don't attract bugs? They need to apply that technology to headlamps. Since the light source is right by your face, sometimes you end up with a cloud of bugs around your face.

Also, I thought I'd list out some of the top trail food stops. The foods hikers want in town are burgers, pastries (like cinnamon rolls), beer, and ice cream. Me, I'm a sucker for a breakfast buffet. So with that in mind I'm gonna list for you the best burgers and breakfast buffets on the trail.

Best Burgers

1. The Gutbuster in Sierra City

Yup, I may draw some heat for this, but this is number one on my list. Massive 1 lb patty, and condiments sliced to order from the deli case. And at $10, it's the best value on the list as well.

2. JJ's Cafe in Old Station

While the Gutbuster wins for value, JJ's wins for flavor. Everything here is made from scratch and it shows. The brioche style bun is baked in house, and the patties are made from local beef. Grab a tray of fresh cinnamon rolls as you leave for a snack later on down the trail.

3. Paradise Valley Cafe, on Hwy 74 south of Idyllwild

With unique flavor combinations, excellent hiker friendly atmosphere (you can sleep on their patio!), and close proximity to the trail, Paradise makes spot number three. Many northbounders put this at number one on their lists, but I think that's due to the fact that it's their first burger on the trail.

4. Yaks in Dunsmuir

Not a popular hiker destination, this is my favorite "undiscovered" trail burger stop. A bit pricey, but the most extensive and unique burger list on the trail.

Best all-you-can-eat breakfast buffets

1. Timberline Lodge, at the base of Mt. Hood

Hands down best breakfast buffet on the trail. Everything is made from scratch in house, including the granola, yogurt, sausage, and baked goods, and there is an extensive and delicious line of hot and cold options. Many hikers do their biggest mileage day coming in to Timberline to make sure to get their money's worth.

2. Drakesbad Ranch, in Lassen National Park

Drakesbad lets hikers "clean out" the buffet after the ranch guests have eaten. Best French toast on the trail, with house made berry compote, sausage, and eggs, then all the hot cereal, fruit, yogurt, and scones you can eat. With your meal comes access to the hotspring-fed pool, laundry, and showers.

3. Callahans, on I-5 near Ashland

If you get the whole hiker package (dinner buffet, laundry, shower, camping on the grass, and breakfast buffet) it's a bit pricey, but the breakfast buffet is worth its price. Fruit, eggs, sausage, juice, then eat pancakes to your heart's content.

4. Sunday breakfast at Kennedy Meadows (south)

While the other buffets will set you back $15, come into Kennedy Meadows on a Sunday for sausage, eggs, fruit, juice, then all the blueberry or chocolate chip pancakes you can eat for just $10.

5. Seiad Valley Cafe 5 -b Challenge

While not TECHNICALLY an all-you-can-eat buffet, only like two people have finished this so I think it deserves an honorable mention. A pizza tray filled with five enormous pancakes. Seiad Valley's claim to fame.

Stay classy, folks, and I'll report back in in a couple days, by which point I should "officially" be a thru hiker.

why hello campo, i've been expecting you...

october 20, 2015

I told you guys about Paradise Valley Cafe – those people were pretty cool. After dinner they let me sleep on their patio before feeding me some French toast and sending me on my way.

Cruising through the desert and past the town of Anza I continued to pass nifty water cache/hang-out spots. I love the names people come up with for the little hiker areas that landowners establish where the trails come close to their property. I really wish I could remember some of them!

Then I came to a place in the middle of nowhere, a place I'd heard about from some north bounders all the way up by Shasta – "Mike's Place." Mike Herrera has a house, presumably off the grid, in the middle of the mountains there, with a water tank that he makes available to hikers. Earlier in the season, he also hosts them and feeds them, but for a south-bounder the status of these types of places becomes pretty uncertain.

I got to the water tank about 6:30p, right as it was getting dark, and filled my bottles. There were no areas nearby where I could camp, and there was a sign (ironically near a closed gate and a "No Trespassing" sign) that said they were home and directed hikers to come on down and rest their feet. So I did. And thus commenced the creepiest night of the trip. The place seemed abandoned, but the pathway was lit by little solar lanterns. No one was home, but there were signs directing hikers in, and it was clear sometime in the recent past this place had hosted many hikers. Not having any other place to go, I gingerly rolled out my bag on the covered porch, ate dinner, and went to sleep. But not before trying (and failing) to text my sister where I was in case something went bad that night. Starting a few hours later, and continuing every hour for the rest of the night, was the scariest creepiest animal noise I've ever heard. It was something like a cross between a bark, and a whine, and someone (yes, someone not something) screaming for help, sounding like it was coming from just on the other side of the house. It really freaked me out at first, but it never got any closer, and sometimes would get more distant, so I tried to sleep. Next morning I got out of there pretty quick.

I've certainly become less and less picky about where I sleep.

Here's "Malibu East." This one had a little "Free Library" and some postcards.

Next day brought with it a big milestone – my last resupply! I had asked mom to put in some fun celebratory snacks, because I'd heard that Warner Springs would have no services. Boy did I hear right! It still puzzles me – Warner Springs is a town of 1500 people with a school and a post office, and there is not a single gas station, grocery store, vending machine, convenience store, anything. Talking to the locals, sounds like they either have to drive 30 miles to Temecula, or 30 miles to Ramona for the nearest gas and food. The town used to mostly consist of a hot springs and golf resort, but that went bankrupt a number of years back and the new owner is taking quite

180

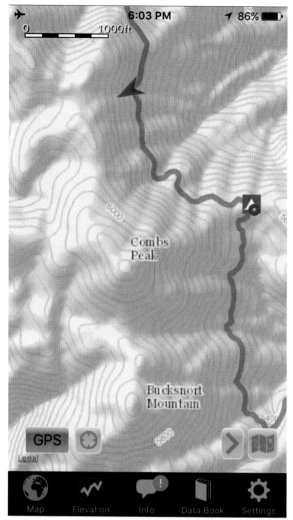

Comb's Peak? More like [Peak Diddy](#). Saw this geographical feature just north of Mike's place and chuckled. When I sent this screen cap to my sister, her favorite part of it was "Buttsnort Mountain."

So many unusual signs! I guess we're far enough south here that they don't feel a need to post this same warning in English. Or maybe they don't care enough about the English speakers to warn them of the apparent danger. Google tells me this says something like "Care! Do not expose your life to the elements. It is not worth it! No drinking water."

In May 2009 a Marine Super Cobra attack helicopter crashed near PCT mile 32.6. Munitions carried by the helicopter were scattered as a result of the crash, and so now there are these very reassuring signs on the trail.

a long time to renovate and get it back on its feet.

I've learned on the trail that having packages delivered to the post office for "general delivery" (i.e. pick up at the counter) is a gamble. In larger towns it's fairly safe because they have long hours (8a-5p, M-F, with some Saturday hours), but small towns are often only 11a-3p M-F, with only maybe a one hour window on Saturday. There have been times in towns I've shown up on Sunday, thinking it was Monday, and times when I've shown up at 4p, only to find the window closed at 3p, and in these cases the only option is to spend the night and wait until midday the next day. The post office was my only option in Warner Springs, however, so I made sure to

Okay, this might be my new favorite trail sign. Recognize that font? That font was originally [developed for use by computers](#), to be printed in magnetic ink. The odd lumpy character shapes give each letter or number a unique signature when scanned by a reader head. The same technology is used at the bottom of checks. And seeing it on a trail sign? This person definitely was a nerd with a sense of humor.

plan my schedule so I'd show up on Monday towards the middle of the day to ensure I'd find an open post office. I was so proud of myself until I walked into the lobby only to find out...that Monday was Columbus Day, and the post office was closed. They do, however, have a "community/resource center" where hikers can hang out during the day and camp outside of at night, so I did that. This last couple hundred miles had turned into quite the relaxing stroll, with plenty of breaks and easy days. A nice change.

One thing that wasn't nice, though, was the fact that once I left Warner Springs I'd have to walk through the last long water carry – 32.7 miles. Dang. I thought I was done with all those, but oh well. At this point I was getting pretty good at "cameling up," and guzzling a couple liters of water at once before dry stretches, so I took a chance, decided to count on a water cache being stocked halfway through, and set off with 4 liters of water. The gamble paid off, and I made it through, after refilling at the Third Gate water cache.

As I descended down through the San Felipe hills, down towards Scissors Crossing, I came to see how the desert can be beautiful. No, it still wasn't beautiful, but I could see how it could be. All along the trail for that stretch were lots of different varieties of cactus, yucca plants, and other new unknown to me varieties of plants. I could imagine how colorful the hillside would be when these were all in bloom in the spring.

And I was running a bit ahead of schedule, so I made a sudden decision to hitch a ride into the old mining town of Julian, now known for its apples and pies instead of gold. Rumor had it that there was a shop in town that gave out free pie and ice cream to hikers, which turned out to be mostly true. Actually, they gave me free pie, ice cream, AND fresh apple cider. Couldn't believe it! And this was the only time on the entire trip that I was asked for my thru hiker permit.

After the most difficult hitch of the trip, standing on the outskirts of Julian for 30 minutes, I finally got a ride back to the trail and continued south through a brutally hot stretch back up into the next clump of mountains. That day I made it all the way to Sunrise Trailhead, and what had started as I descended the San Felipe hills continued and the desert became more and more beautiful. I'm sure the plants and landscape became more beautiful, but what I really noticed is the sky. For the past nearly four months I have looked up to a barren sky – rarely have I seen any clouds. And unfortunately this has meant that,

While I was in Julian, they had a delivery of a couple of these carts full of white sugar, brown sugar, and flour. That's a lot of baking supplies...

See? This could be pretty cool! If the flowers were blooming...

The last day started with heavy fog, which I loved. Also, it made the spider webs really stand out because they gathered all the moisture on their strands.

Sunrise at Sunrise Trailhead.

I spent my last night on the trail at Lake Morena, ready for the final push to the southern terminus. This was a fun night, because since the ground was too hard for stakes, I made a "fort" out of my tarp and a picnic table to protect me from the imminent thunderstorms.

combined with the typical forest cover, I haven't been able to enjoy many marvelous sunsets. But oh my! The sky began to fill with clouds, and as the trail traversed along high ridges with expansive views of the desert to the east, I got a front row seat to watch thunderstorms north of me (where I'd just been) and well east of me. Clouds are so amazing and intriguing, I think if I'd had clouds to watch while hiking the trail, I'd never have been bored while walking. They look, at the same time, both so hard and so soft. When lightning lights them up from within, they look like a stellar factory from which I expect starships to emerge. And when the sun comes up behind them, I feel like I'm in a magical painting.

The next evening found me at Mt. Laguna, and in the forest again. A light rain as I walked into town gave me an excuse to pull out my umbrella, but luckily it didn't cool down so much as to remove my craving for ice cream at the general store there. Mt. Laguna would be a cool place if the shops were open, but even though their signs all said they should be open at 4p, they were all closed. I guess it really is the off season.

On that last day, that last push to the end, I had a cool idea. I thought it would be fun to take a picture facing directly south every time I cut the distance between me and the border in half. But then I realized that would be an infinite number of pictures and I would never get to the border. So I decided against that and just did what I always do, you know, take pictures of interesting or weird stuff along the way.

And then, like everything else I've encountered in the desert, the end hit me before I expected it. It was just like right there! About a half mile from the end, my best

friend's mom was waiting for me, walking up the trail to meet me, and had champagne and ice cream waiting at the finish! Also means I got my own personal photographer to immortalize my last few steps 😄

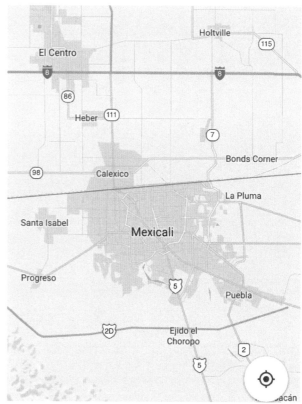

So I was looking around the map and I found this. Now, I've definitely heard of Mexicali before, and thought it was clever, but I didn't know that it had a partner town on the other side of the border called Calexico. I love seeing stuff like this. It gives me hope that the world isn't as serious as I'm afraid it is sometimes.

Like I've said a few times before, I've had lots of time to think. As I've gotten closer to the end of my journey, more and more people have asked me if I've come to any realizations or conclusions. If the knotty problems of life have somehow sorted themselves out simply through many hours of gradually untangling them in my head. If I've somehow become "enlightened."

I think I *have* reached a conclusion.

I've thought about what the meaning of adventure is, I've pondered the effects of fear and uncertainty on our ability to achieve our goals, I've contemplated the different effects on a person between society and the wild. I've become more in tune with my body. And yes, I have reached a conclusion.

My feet hurt. Like, really hurt.

Yup, that's my conclusion. But because of that I can learn so much more – after countless hours of mulling over life's issues, approaching them from every direction, and arriving at no solid conclusions other than that my feet hurt, I know that I'm not a philosopher. Some people are incredibly skilled at understanding their own motivations and forming road maps of where to go in life and how best to get there. But that's not me. Sitting around thinking and planning and digesting isn't going to get me anywhere. I accomplish things best when I just go, and see what comes to me.

Every year, as I try and "decide" what my next adventure might be, I look back to the past year and note that I had NO IDEA that this year would bring the adventure it did. And that gives me hope that even though I don't have a good idea what the next year (or five or ten) will hold, it'll be something I'd have never imagined. And in a way, that allows me to not feel compelled to plan. If I force something, and make a plan just so I can have a plan to follow, I might be precluding some other adventure that might have come along. Because, after all, if I make a plan, the adventure is something that me right now in my current state of growth and understanding knew and understood. If I wait and see what happens, I can grow and mature because the adventures that come to me may be something my current self could not have imagined, could not have understood, and I'll have to rise to the occasion.

As I sit here in San Diego, now done with the longest adventure I've ever set out on, how have a I changed? By the end of the long hot stretch that is Southern California, I'm sure I took on what hikers call "the look" – not quite dazed, or jaded, or tired, or distant, or hard, but somehow a combination of all of those. I'd finally achieved hiker zen. In those last 200 miles I would voluntarily pass up town food to eat my hiker food, and I might just as easily have eaten granola bars for dinner as hot food cooked on my camp stove. I would walk the entire day with no breaks, plowing along for hours and hours arriving into camp much earlier than I used to, and having hiked more miles. And the hiker hunger I had earlier in the hike had abated, leaving me with a remarkably reasonable appetite.

But apart from the physical, things seem so much less urgent and strict than they used to. I've always been the kind of person to love planning, love certainty, and hate germs. And it's been a long process, but I see myself relaxing a bit. Food for a 5-day stretch which used to be obsessively planned is now haphazardly thrown into a bag, water reports which used to be pored over to determine the exact amount of life sustaining fluid required to get me through the next section are now more of a guide just to make sure I'm not making a huge mistake. My cook pot hasn't been washed in months, and I don't make the obsessive effort to wash my clothes in bathroom sinks with hand soap anymore. Many things that used to be their own end are now just means to an end.

How have I not changed? I've always been a practical person, and all these things I've just described have had the effect of making me more practical. I still have trouble seeing the magic in things. Someone once told me they didn't want to know show stars work or the secrets behind things in nature, because that takes the magic away. That's never been me, because I find it interesting to investigate things and learn about them. But that means no magic, because magic means allowing yourself to not know.

chapter 3: wheels again
east coast road trip

we ain't finished yet

october 23, 2015

I hope y'all don't think that just because I got to Campo I'm done adventuring. I had another thing on my list, and the timing worked out pretty well for it. So – if you guys want to join me for an "after party," I'll keep posting for a bit longer.

Let's start with a cool song by George Ezra, "Blame It On Me": http://youtu.be/mCjYB3rAJ6w

My "host family" the Edwalls put me up from the time I finished the trail (Saturday) to the day of my flight (Tuesday), and in the time between we had a blast! I got to drive my old motorcycle that is now finding new life in their garage (who remembers that lime green ninja??), we played Scrabble and Monopoly, and I was invited out on a super chill bike ride around San Diego, past Marine World and along Pacific Beach. Finally, I got a ride to the airport in a vintage convertible Porsche Speedster!

But my flight didn't go back home. Well, not directly. First, I'm making a detour out to New England to check out (by car!) some of the mountains and trail towns along the Appalachian Trail, and catch some views of the New England fall colors, since they're peaking so late this year. I hope to also get to celebrate with my uncle in Connecticut on Nov 4 (Election Day!) since he'll be running for his fourth term on the school board.

My flight got into JFK pretty late, so after spending the night in the airport waiting area (earplugs and a bandana eyemask were essential), I picked up a car and headed north.

My home for the next two weeks will be a red Prius, and after $17.25 in tolls, I made it somewhere north of Portland, Maine the first night to park for the night with me in it.

Oh! I also tried mead at a small brewery in Portland for the first time, quite tasty! Portland has a LOT of breweries. Surprised me.

Airport sleeping, how cozy!

188

The next morning I got a bright and early start. Well, dark and early. The days of course are getting shorter for the season, which I'm used to, but they're even shorter this far north. I get daylight from 7a-6p, so I gotta make it count. Going north past Portland I took the coastal scenic route, bypassing Augusta (one of the two big cities in Maine, along with Portland) – it was a good choice. This was the stretch with the best fall colors, and freeways are boring anyway. Also along this stretch was my favorite town here in Maine, a small town named Camden.

My plan is to roughly parallel the Appalachian Trail, so the first stop was Millinocket, the town closest to the northern end of the trail at Mt. Katahdin in Baxter State Park.

I couldn't actually climb Katahdin, since the weather was bad and it's pretty much past the safe season for summiting. But I did drive through the Debsconeag Lakes Wilderness on the southern border of the park on an intermittently paved road and along the Nesowadnehunk Deadwater in Penobscot County. No joke, I couldn't make up these names. Then the road turned into a pretty rough logging road, with some fords.

But my Prius was a champ throughout the 2-hour pummeling. I stopped briefly to take a dayhike out to the First Debsconeag Lake, and got to experience some of the differences between AT trail and PCT trail.

The forests here are like nothing I've ever seen before, densely packed and with narrow trunks. It's temperate rainforest that forms a solid canopy, and fills the trail with slippery roots. Trail blazes are painted on the trees incredibly frequently, like every 25-50 feet since the trail is so rough and the forest is so dense. Rarely does the trail go above tree line, and when it does there aren't the vast expansive views that you get in the Cascades and the Sierras.

This wild and dense forest gives me the sense of total isolation and remoteness, but unique to this forest is I get the sense of antiquity. When I got to the lake overlook, I couldn't help but imagine that I was one of the original French fur traders in the early 17th century, traveling overland through uncharted forests and waterways. There's some truth to this – apparently it is an ancient(ish) forest, with some sections having totally escaped logging and having trees up to 300 years old.

Back on the road, after a short detour/wrong turn, I

Hours of this! With the occasional scenic water crossing.

It's so...tempting, lol.

Google gave me no indication this "road" wouldn't be paved for 75 miles. Or that it would be filled with miniature lakes.

189

All of Maine feels so wild and remote. I can't properly convey it with a picture. But here's the First Debsconeag Lake.

This is where it's AT! Okay, bad joke.

These are called the "Ice Caves." Would've been welcome if it had been a hot day.

made my way south to the White Mountains, where I'll be camping at an AT trailhead and checking out Mt. Washington tomorrow.

So Maine is a pretty cool place. It introduces itself to drivers as "vacationland" and "the way life SHOULD be," and drivers are greeted by unusual signs, like "high incidence of moose accidents next six miles, use caution." The trees range from the deepest reds I've ever seen on a tree to rich green – a stunning range of hues. The main industries seem to be cottages, B&Bs, and small hotels, and art. I'm impressed at the amount of services for the very low population density – there are churches (white steepled, of course), McDonalds, and full supermarkets like every few miles. I exaggerate, but it is impressive.

Some low fog set in just before sunset to make it really pretty.

The other thing that struck me was that on the west coast, and most of the US, society has forced wilderness into nice neat contained areas called national parks and national forests. In Maine, it's the opposite – the wilderness has forced people into nice neat contained areas called towns. In between towns is wild untamed forest. Tons of it. And lakes. On the coast are so many towns that are just classic New England, and it appears that not much has changed since the early parts of the century, though I know it has. They have kept the old coal power plants with the giant smokestacks, all the architecture is original, and the forest is as menacing and mysterious as when Lewis and Clark first set out to explore the west.

Full picture album here: https://flic.kr/s/aHskjfPA8e

1500 miles and counting

Just gotta say, good thing this rental car has unlimited mileage. Definitely getting my money's worth.

So. You know when you pull a leftover container out of the fridge and the food inside is covered with a patchwork of mold spots in all different colors? And you're not sure what's underneath it all, except that it's generally lumpy?

That's what the mountains here remind me of, with their fall colors. But don't worry, not in a bad way – they look pretty, they just remind me of moldy unrecognizable food. The hills aren't enormous, just enough to give the countryside a lumpy topography. And the many colors of trees give the hillsides a mottled, fuzzy texture. But trust me, it is pretty. I figured I haven't stunned you in awhile with a bad analogy, so I'd better get it out of the way.

So when I left you last, I was headed south out of Maine, and that night camped in the White Mountains of New Hampshire. Now of course I use the term "camped" loosely, as since its been rainy and windy and freezing at night what I've actually been doing is parking at AT trailheads and sleeping in the car. Camping at the trailheads in the evenings also sets me up perfectly to do little day hikes in the morning along the AT to wake up with the fresh morning air, and that morning I walked a couple miles in along the Rattle River to see my first AT shelter.

The Appalachian Trail is different from the PCT in that there are shelters all along it to camp in, ranging from primitive lean-tos to something like hostels, I've been told, especially in the White Mountains. You hear all kinds of stories about them, about how nasty they are, how full of mice they are (like someone who knew a guy that woke up with a mouse in his boxers), but after learning about myth and legend on the PCT, I'm inclined to think they probably aren't that bad.

The White Mountains are home to what are affectionately know to hikers as "the prezzies" – that is, the Presidential Range of mountains (as you can guess, each of the peaks in the range is named after a president). Among them was the next place I wanted to check out, Mt. Washington. New Hampshire, though only home to a few miles of the AT, has the most miles of the trail above treeline of any state, as the trail meanders along the prezzies. These mountains are unique, though, in that they are notorious for the worst weather in the United States. Mt. Washington has about a hundred days a year of winds above hurricane force at the summit (greater than 75 mph), and holds the record for fastest recorded wind anywhere on earth, 231 mph. Unfortunately, the road to drive up closed for the season on October 18, so I just missed it. Dangers of off-season traveling I guess 😔

You guys have all heard me rave about Darn Tough socks, right? Well, they're made in Vermont, and I thought it'd be a blast if I could tour their factory near Montpelier, but when I called, the representative said that they were renovating and upgrading the factory so I couldn't. But on a whim I asked her if she could recommend any maple farms to check out in the area, and she gave me one to check out. So, I got to go learn about maple syrup. Vermont produces about 40% of the syrup in the US, but each tree only produces about 1/3 to 1/2 of a gallon of syrup per season since it takes 40-50 gallons of sap to make a gallon of syrup. The trees are tapped in winter, then sap is harvested in spring when the sugar shacks then become busy boiling it down from 1% sugar to 66% sugar. During the fall they're just in full-time tourist entertainment mode. I learned something else, though, this time about marketing: they were selling a treat called a "maple creemee" which I just had to try to see what it was. Turns out it's just maple flavored soft serve ice cream in a cone. So I learned when selling something standard, name it something unusual so people have to buy it just to figure out what it is.

Around this time I had contacted a friend I'd made in New Zealand who lived in Massachusetts (which I can now spell without the aid of autocorrect!) and asked for some recommendations. At his suggestion I headed up to Camel's Hump State Park, and severely underestimating both the distance and how strenuous the climb would be, summited just at dark and with the top engulfed in a

Finally got some good sunshine to make the colors "pop."

The Rattle River shelter. The whole side facing the camera is open, and there are two hikers "bombing" my photo, asleep in their bags. The AT reminds me a lot of the trails in NZ, in foliage, and weather, and the presence of shelters like this.

Very pleasant conditions up top as I drove by, dontcha think?

freezing cloud with lots of wind. I pulled out my phone to take a picture, but with my dexterity severely compromised by the freezing wind, I dropped my phone and finally broke the screen.

So I headed back down without much celebration and camped (you know, "parked") at the trailhead for the night. This time I had company, and was joined by two other road tripping groups with the same idea.

New Hampshire and Vermont were quite a bit different from Maine – they actually had cities, and paved roads, and industries besides tourism. They raise cattle, grow hay, make lots and lots of furniture judging by all the signs, and of course Vermont is known for white cheddar and maple syrup. They also have mountains and clearings in the forest from which to see up to those mountains and down from them. The towns are still distinctly New England, all the houses white with wooden siding, and small white steepled churches in every town. Vermont was home to my favorite New England town, Rutland, which I figured to be small enough to be pleasant, big enough to be livable, new enough to have modern conveniences but old enough to be quaint, and just the right amount of hipster.

Some recommended places in Massachusetts had been Greylock Peak and the Mohawk Trail, so I figured those into my drive south. Greylock Peak is the tallest point in Massachusetts, at a piddly 3400', which made me chuckle. But it does give you a good view east towards Boston.

Having seen lots of postings at the general stores in small towns the last few days for harvest dinners and festivals on Saturday the 24th, and it finally being Saturday the 24th, I started looking for one in each small town in Mass I passed through. But as is usually the case, once you start looking for something, it seems to be impossible to find. So I settled for Chinese food instead, and "camped" at October Mountain State Forest. Lame.

Massachusetts overall gave me the impression of being very affluent. Also, more "matter-of-fact" and less cutesy, if that makes any sense. Still white wooden house architecture, but bigger houses, and more of them. The terrain was much flatter in general, and the forests and state parks were small and numerous rather than few and large like the other states so far.

The next section promised to be an adventure for sure! I had tried to find some churches while hiking the PCT, but I rarely found myself in a town with a church on a

Looking out from Camel's Hump. Quite a view, isn't it?

This is the last picture I took before my phone screen took on the appearance of a spider web and I had to be very careful swiping to avoid getting glass splinters.

More "green tunnel" (well, yellow tunnel now) leading up to the top of the "mountain."

View of Massachusetts from Greylock Peak.

Sunday. This Sunday, however, I was a stone's throw from Albany, New York. I found a small church in a suburb of Albany, and after the service was invited to someone's house for lunch and then later to their small group in the evening. That evening, I was offered a bed and meals. I was so surprised and overwhelmed, the young family who hosted me was incredibly sweet and generous.

I was super excited to check out upstate New York too, because all I know about New York is Manhattan. But of course there's so much more! I mean, obviously they love their "A" mountain ranges (Allegheny, Adirondack, and Appalachian), but they have Niagara Falls, Buffalo (the home of Buffalo wings!), and more "big" cities than any of the New England states I'd been through so far. I definitely see the truth now in their slogan "The Empire State," and it took seeing that on a license plate frame to realize that's why "The Empire State Building" is called what it is. Even excluding New York City, and even Albany, driving through Utica, Syracuse, and Saratoga Springs, you get a much more industrial big city sense than any of the other New England states. All the architecture in New York is brick, with a very industrial revolution feel. As you head south and west, the landscape transitions from the dense forests of the northern states to the rolling grassy hills of Pennsylvania, with the occasional Amish horse-drawn carriage to boot. Side note: somehow, Google maps pronounces "Schenectady" flawlessly and without hesitation, but struggles with the word "diamond." Oh, and apparently there's a suburb of Albany that isn't very nice, called Troy, but locals refer to it as "the Troy-let" and that makes me smile.

Backcountry upstate New York is full of lakes, and I guess at some point they ran out of names – west of Saratoga Springs is a chain of lakes named First Lake through Eighth Lake.

New York is a big state by New England standards – I took the scenic route up and around, but it took me like nine hours to get from Albany to Niagara Falls. Niagara Falls is supposed to be a state park, preserved against encroaching commercialism, but man it sure feels like a giant theme park with huge hotels, casinos, souvenir shops, and ticket booths. At least you can walk past them and get unobstructed views of the falls. They're so epic, they make you feel so small. Really a wonderful and mesmerizing experience.

And of course, as I mentioned earlier, when in Buffalo, how can I not stop in and try the original Buffalo wings

And, just like the Empire State Building with its antennas, or a girl with high heels, they cheated a bit and put a really tall monument on top of Greylock Peak to add a few extra feet. Or maybe it's "just" a war memorial.

This is what most of northern New York looks like, before you head south and west along the Erie Canal area out to Buffalo.

at Anchor Bar? There's no doubt they're authentic. No fanfare, no newfangled flavors like teriyaki or garlic parmesan, no options like breaded or naked. You tell them how hot you want em, and whether you want 10, 20, or 50 of em. Done. They really are the best wings I've had, not pretentious at all.

My host family from Albany made a big impression on me. I love seeing young families around my age (late twenties, early thirties), with a young kid or two, really being a part of their church community, taking a leadership role and leading a small group study, and looking to God for direction in their lives. It is the most amazing blessing when you're a wandering traveler to be welcomed into a loving home. That is something I want for my life – to be a part of a church community, to be

settled down enough to welcome visitors into my home and take care of them, help mentor them. But historically that's been really difficult for me, to stay a part of the same community long enough to really build roots and strong relationships. I feel like this is a very useful part of my life though, to build enough life experiences that I can help people and relate to people and provide advice.

This is just HALF of the falls – America Falls. To the right is Horseshoe Falls. But if you look right, all the casinos and hotels on the Canadian side creep into the pic.

Anchor Bar, creator of Buffalo wings. A++, would eat again.

i've got time

november 23, 2015

Hey guys, it's been a while. Once I got home I got distracted and didn't ever put up a last post, but I have some more pictures for you. In case you're curious, here's a map of my route through the east coast ▶

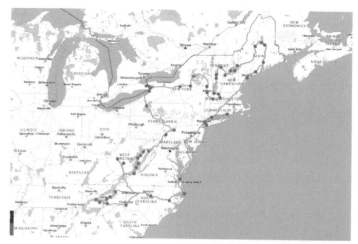

The last 3000 miles of the road trip had a couple more neat things in store. Having already seen the typical Pennsylvania sights of Philadelphia (which, by the way, is the only World Heritage City in the United States, and the fifth most populous city in the U.S.) and Amish country, I couldn't pass up checking out Hershey, PA on my way through (especially since the chocolate tour was free!). To me, and I'm sure many others, the Hershey brand has become synonymous with inexpensive candy and average quality chocolate, but learning about its history I was impressed by its origin story. The town of Hershey wasn't the result of some recent publicity stunt by the modern-day giant corporation, it was built for the workers at the same time the plant was built, in 1909, to provide entertainment and tax-free services to the employees. Milton sounded like quite a good guy, really focusing on the well being of his workers, and was the first to come up with a way to mass-produce milk chocolate. In addition, he established a school for orphans in the town since he was unable to have children of his own, and donated his estate and 30% of all future Hershey profits to the school. Since the company grew to become America's largest chocolate company after his death, the Milton Hershey School is now one of the richest schools in the world providing free education, health care, and counseling to thousands of orphans.

Even though I've been on the road quite a bit, I'm not sure I'm past a million miles yet, so I still have to wear my seatbelt. This sign was part of a quirky safety campaign by the Pennsylvania Department of Transportation.

However, business is business, and it seems to me that it's impossible to maintain one man's vision for generations afterwards in a multi-billion dollar corporation. The informational panels on the chocolate tour tried to highlight current efforts of the company to source fair-trade cocoa and other positive aspects, but neglected to tell the tourists that the Hershey Company, along with Nestlé, lobbied the FDA recently to change the legal definition of "chocolate" to allow the use of partially hydrogenated vegetable oils in place of cocoa butter, and artificial sweeteners and milk substitutes.

The next day, after camping in Michaux State Forest, I kept heading south, and made a spur-of-the-moment decision to veer off-route and follow signs for some random place called "Lost River State Park" in West Virginia.

So this was the free part. But I didn't realize there's also a theme park (with roller coasters) and a stadium.

When I got there, I realized I had lost cell reception, and since I was off route, I had no idea where I was or where I was heading…so I just kept driving. I was ironically lost in Lost River. On a windy one-lane mountain road. For like an hour. And it was pretty cool, cause I knew I'd get to a somewhat major road at some point. And if the road dead-ended I would just turn around. Sure is nice to have time.

I did eventually get to a two lane road, and continued south into an absolutely enormous national forest complex consisting of the Monongahela, George Washington, and Jefferson National Forests that spans the whole height of Virginia. Passed Seneca Rocks, Seneca Caverns, Green Bank National Radio Observatory, and camped near some random place named Catawba.

I didn't know what else to do in West Virginia (seriously, what else is there to do in West Virginia?) so I was just going to keep going south to meet my Uncle in Raleigh, NC. But then I decided it would be fun to see Charleston, WV. And like I said, I've got time, right? So next day I detoured over to Charleston, the capital of WV. And it was cool I guess. On the way back east, I stopped in to the New River Gorge, home to the New River Gorge Bridge (imagine that!), which is the longest single span arch bridge in the Western Hemisphere. And then I realized what West Virginia is known for (and no, it's not the plethora of strip clubs and adult stores I saw billboards for)…it's known for coal! So I totally wanted to tour a coal mine, but realized I no longer had enough time…had to get to Raleigh.

In Raleigh I got to celebrate my uncle's birthday, and see my cousin's new house. And it really rubbed in the fact that everyone I know my age is getting married and buying a house. And I'm getting old, lol. But again, as I've said before, I've got time, right? Starting to sense a theme here.

After Raleigh was what I was looking forward to as one of the highlights of my trip – Asheville. I've heard so much about Asheville, and on paper it seems to meet a lot of the criteria I've been looking for in a city – small enough to be manageable, big enough to provide services and activities, small enough to be nestled in the mountains, but large enough to not be a small mountain town, home to a university, a reasonable amount of snow in the winter, and a moderate summer. And it is all those things, for sure, but after spending Halloween evening in downtown Asheville, I'm thinking maybe I don't fit in with the college-age hippies anymore. As I said, I'm get-

Hershey's Chocolate World is home to the entire line of Hershey's candies, including these ridiculous 1/2 pound Reese's peanut butter cups that are the size of my hand. I offered to bring some home to my mom to hand out for Halloween, she said no.

Pennsylvania had some creepy roads. This one was evil.

Falling Spring Falls, just north of Covington, Virginia. In Thomas Jefferson's time, this used to be a 200ft tall waterfall, but limestone mining operations necessitated "relocating" it to its current location, where it is now only 80ft.

Saw this cool retro sign in the hipster district of Charleston, the East End, after having lunch at Tricky Fish. For some reason, it simultaneously reminds of my dad's old Datsun and Back to the Future.

For as small and simple of a state capital as Charleston is, it had a very beautiful capitol building.

The New River Gorge Bridge. This thing is massive. And the name is a little misleading – there's no "old" river bridge that this replaced. The river is simply named the New River.

ting old 😫 But this brings up practical aspects to cities that I sometimes neglect – there have to be jobs there. And the job market in Asheville isn't great, it doesn't sound like.

Leaving the next morning through thick fog on the Blue Ridge Parkway, I didn't get any great views from atop Mt. Mitchell, but it cleared enough to enjoy the rest of my time in the mountains before heading east again to the coast. I had just over a day to get from North Carolina back up to Connecticut to celebrate another uncle's local school board election win.

Oooooohhhh but you know me, I couldn't go straight there. First, I had to check out Kitty Hawk. So Kitty Hawk is on the coast, I think a lot of people know that, but I didn't know that it's on a cool geographic feature called the "Outer Banks" – a narrow strip of land (between 1/4 to 1/2 mile wide) miles offshore from NC that spans the whole height of NC. I'd read all about it at the free natural history museum in downtown Raleigh. The outer banks is also where Roanoke Island is located – home to the "Lost Colony" of Roanoke – and Ocracoke Island, the last refuge of Edward Teach (the famous pirate "Blackbeard").

And then…and then I headed north, across the Chesapeake Bay Bridge-Tunnel (which is technically called the Lucius J. Kellam Jr. Bridge–Tunnel, but no one calls it that). It was a bit out of my way, but how could I not? The CBBT is one of only 10 combination bridge-tunnels in the world – yup, you heard that right, combination bridge/tunnel. It starts as a regular low trestle bridge, then at two man-made islands in the middle of the Chesapeake bay, it dives underground into undersea tunnels, emerging one mile later at two more man-made islands. And then, on the north end, it climbs up and becomes a high-level bridge so ships can pass underneath. So I imagine this is one of the few bridges in the world that ships can pass both over AND under.

All told, I think it cost like $60 in tolls to get from North Carolina to Connecticut, so I'm glad I had stopped at the ATM before heading north. Still don't understand why toll booths don't take credit cards.

One of those tolls was to cross the George Washington Bridge, just above Upper Manhattan. And wow, just wow. Crossing the Harlem River was absolutely mind-blowing. I don't think I've ever seen so many freeways stacked, so many interchanges tangled in so small a space, woven in and around buildings, with such ridicu-

On the drive to Asheville the road went through a beautiful gorge that passed a few waterfalls. Looking Glass Falls, Cullasaja Falls, and pictured here is Bridal Veil Falls, where you can drive behind the falls. So now I'm aware of five waterfalls named Bridal Veil – two in California, one in Oregon, one in Colorado, and one in North Carolina.

My cousin Nick getting some harpoon-throwing practice at Mystic seaport.

lous traffic. I'm accustomed to San Francisco traffic and Los Angeles traffic, but I felt like a completely novice driver – I've never experienced car horns being used as a necessary part of traffic navigation. But I was soon out of thick of it after passing the Bronx and Yonkers, and shortly after that I was in Westport, CT.

Something else I realized while passing through New York City, was that something was wrong with my Prius. The entire trip I'd had trouble tracking down radio stations, so I'd suffered through poor reception and lots of silence during the many hours of driving as a result. I'd chalked it up to radio signals not carrying well through the thick forest of the east coast, and the spread out

rural backroads I'd been traveling on. But even here, in the most densely and numerously populated area in the United States, I was having trouble tracking down radio stations. So finally I checked the antenna the next time I stopped. And I found the problem. The antenna was missing. Oh well 😵

It was great to see family in Connecticut, and learn a little about the business world from my Uncle. We took a day trip out to Mystic Seaport, and had pizza at Mystic Pizza, which is apparently famous for being the location of a famous movie that was before my time. And I almost got to tour a nuclear submarine, but it's closed on Tuesdays 😆

I'll leave you guys with one last thought. On the flight back, as the plane flew across California, I saw a different landscape. No, it was the same physical landscape I'd seen dozens of times on flights before, but somehow it meant something more now. I've had my nose in maps so much the last few months, and seen so many different

Clingman's Dome, in the Great Smoky Mountains, is the highest point in the GSM as well as the highest point on the Appalachian Trail. However, even at this point the mountains aren't high enough to get above tree line, so they've built a giant observation tower with a big circular ramp.

Me and my cousins about to eat famous Mystic Pizza.

Flying over the freshly dusted mountains just east of Mono Lake, in Nevada.

landscapes, and spent so much time *living in nature*, I felt like I had a real connection to this landscape now. In the same way that a picture of someone you know is so much more meaningful and somehow contains so much more information than a picture of a stranger, so now the mountains were *my mountains*. I recognized the peaks and troughs, the shapes and lakes. Instead of having to search for recognizable landmarks as I have in the past flying over, I just…understood the landscape. And they jumped out at me. Mono Lake! Tioga Pass! Hetch Hetchy! There's New Priest Grade! And when the plane banked right to start heading north, you could look directly east, deep into the Sierras through the long, straight canyons inhabited by the Stanislaus and Mokelumne Rivers.

Maybe that's what I got out of this trip – a connection to the world. Maybe that's the difference between observing the world and *experiencing* the world. By experiencing the world you can see that there is still so much magic out there. People talk about pessimists versus optimists, but I think there are *magicists and non-magicists*. Seems to me earthly happiness is inextricably linked to being able to find the magic in things – in the world, in nature, in people – and this is a skill that most children excel at but most people lose as they get older. We need to exercise our imaginations, our creativity, and our curiosity, but that's hard to do if you're in a hurry, if you don't have time. Slow down, find the magic.

Made in the USA
Las Vegas, NV
09 November 2020